Our forbidden land

FAY GODWIN

OUR FORBIDDEN LAND

JONATHAN CAPE LONDON

When you've spent half your political life dealing with humdrum issues like the environment, it's exciting to have a real crisis on your hands.

Margaret Thatcher, 1981, at the time of the Falklands War

The core of Tory philosophy and the case for protecting the environment are the same; no generation has a freehold on this earth; all we have is a life tenancy with a full repairing lease and this Government intends to meet the terms of that lease in full.

Margaret Thatcher, 1988 Conservative Party Conference

We Conservatives are not merely friends of the earth, we are its guardians and trustees.

Margaret Thatcher, 1989, being interviewed by Michael Buerk on Nature, *BBC2*

Our forbidden land
first published 1990
photographs © Fay Godwin 1990
text © Fay Godwin 1990
Jonathan Cape Ltd, 20 Vauxhall Bridge Road
London SW1V 2SA

Fay Godwin has asserted her right to be
identified as the author of this work

a CIP catalogue record for this book
is available from the British Library

ISBN 0-224-02751-4 (hardback)
      0-224-03015-9 (paperback)

designed by Ken Garland and Associates
photoset in Linotron Bembo by
Rowland Phototypesetting Ltd
Bury St Edmunds, Suffolk
printed in Great Britain by
Jackson · Wilson Ltd, Leeds

CONTENTS

ACKNOWLEDGMENTS

Although the views in this book are my own, I could not have done the book without help from many people, far too many to name. But special thanks must go to:

Peter Cattrell and Richard Hamilton for making the prints; Cass Wedd for sensitive and imaginative help with research; David Beskine and Alan Mattingly of the Ramblers' Association for endless patience and help. Chris Hall and Peter Melchett for further assistance in checking, Ken Garland and Associates for bringing order to bear on a forbidding task and David Godwin, my non-related editor, for his support throughout the project.

Thanks also for help and support from Yvonne Anderson, Cliff Dean, Arthur Gemmell, Nicholas Godwin, Pat Gowen, Ernest Hall, Mike Harding, Catherine Heron, Patrick Heron, Paul Hill, Dr John Illingworth, Beverley Penney, Jim Perrin, Michael Pitts, John Riddall, Lady Sylvia Sayer, Clive and Pamela Sheppard, Dr Cyril Smith, Dan Stockwell, Ivy Sutherland, Sir Roland Wade, Bridget Yallop.

Also the Biodynamics Agricultural Research Association, the Council for the Protection of Rural England, English Heritage, the Forestry Commission, Friends of the Earth, Greenham Common Peace Camp, Greenpeace, the Henry Doubleday Research Association, Highland Regional Council, the Imperial War Museum, the London Wildlife Trust, the Ministry of Defence, the National Trust, the National Trust Countryside Protection Group, the Nature Conservancy Council, the Ramblers' Association, the Royal Society for the Protection of Birds; *The Dangers of Organo-Phosphates* Broadsheet from Mark Purdey's *Open Space* film 'Aggro-chemicals' on BBC TV; *Face the Facts*, BBC Radio Four; *The Food Programme*, presented by Derek Cooper on BBC Radio Four; *Nature* presented by Michael Buerk, BBC TV; *The North Sea*, presented by Susannah York, BBC TV; *Panorama*, BBC TV; as well as many more individuals and institutions. My thanks to all.

GLOSSARY

AGR	Advanced gas-cooled reactor
AONB	Area of outstanding natural beauty
BSE	Bovine spongiform encephalitis (scrapie-like 'mad cow disease')
BST	Bovine Somatotrophin, milk-boosting hormone
CAP	Common Agricultural Policy
CEGB	Central Electricity Generating Board
ESA	Environmentally sensitive area
FC	Forestry Commission
LWT	London Wildlife Trust
MAFF	Ministry of Agriculture, Fisheries and Food
MoD	Ministry of Defence
NCC	Nature Conservancy Council
NFU	National Farmers' Union
NT	National Trust
RA	Ramblers' Association
Ramsar	Internationally designated wetland site
RSPB	Royal Society for the Protection of Birds
SSSI	Site of special scientific interest

INTRODUCTION

I was brought up in various far-flung parts of the world, as my father was a diplomat and my mother an American artist, so I spent very little time in England until the early 1950s, and even then I kept travelling to the continent.

I have always loved walking, ever since I can remember. I walked a lot in Austria in my twenties, as well as going on hut-to-hut ski tours, until a shattered leg put a stop to the long-distance walks. Later, I walked on the Sussex Downs with my husband and young children, and still have the delight of walking from time to time with my elder son, but more usually I walk on my own now, with camera.

I had loved the clearly marked paths in the Austrian hills and Alps, but I also liked what I saw of public footpaths in England, especially the fact that I could walk through a domestic farming landscape in the Garden of England and home counties on these paths. I joined the Ramblers' Association in the mid-1950s and have been a member ever since, supporting their efforts to keep these very important paths open, and pressing for more access to the countryside on foot.

I became more aware of paths when I read Wainwright's guides to the Lake District. They were so clear that my twelve-year-old son could choose the walk and map-read, and I spent many more happy hours 'armchair walking'. By this time I had started to take an interest in landscape photography, as opposed to snaps of my family in the landscape. Using Wainwright's guides, however, with their absolute clarity and comprehensive descriptions of all aspects of the walks, even to where one might encounter fierce dogs, or where they might just sound fierce, eventually led to the idea of working on a walkers' guide myself – a good way, I thought, to get out into the landscape while pretending to work. I was introduced to the late J. R. L. Anderson, and together we worked on *The Oldest Road: An Exploration of the Ridgeway*. I walked it many times, while cutting my teeth on landscape work which turned out harder than I had expected. I spent hours at Avebury, where my interest in prehistoric stones and barrows began. Avebury was, and fortunately still is, accessible to the public, but I was often stopped by officious people from the Ministry of Works in whose care Avebury then was. I lost

many pictures, through their red-tape interrogations – they used to interrupt me just when the light was wonderful and take me back to a little office, and each time I had to prove that I was working on the book. It is extraordinary that Government agencies and others so often try to stop us photographing our heritage, our parks and gardens. They seem to think they can censor as well as try to copyright the landscape and our heritage. There are some apposite words in *Walks round Huddersfield* by G. S. Phillips:

'For whoever may own the land, no man can own the beauty of the landscape; at all events no man can exclusively own it. Beauty is a kind of property which cannot be bought, sold or conveyed in any parchment deed, but it is an inalienable common right; and he who carries the true seeing eyes in his head, no matter how poor he may otherwise be, is the legitimate lord of the landscape.'

Although I had trouble photographing Avebury for that first book, I had no problems of physical access, since the Ridgeway was already a long-distance footpath. These surfaced with my next book, *The Drovers' Roads of Wales*, with Shirley Toulson. We both experienced blocked footpaths, vanished footpaths, and farmers, complete with shotgun and a couple of dogs, coming out to ask why we were trespassing. 'This is a public right of way,' we would say. 'That may be, but you're going round by the road,' and in those circumstances we did. A number of paths were also completely blocked off by forestry plantations; Wales is far worse than England for blocked footpaths. I had of course encountered blocked footpaths before, but was now more aware of them since we were trying to do a walkers' guide.

Since then I have had many more encounters with blocked paths, and been denied access to open moorland. One of the most extraordinary occasions was a couple of years ago, up on Ponden Moor near Bradford. My B & B landlady had suggested I take a walk up a particular valley through the moors, to get some good views for photographs. I came back through a farmyard next to the B & B. 'Have you been up on the moor?' the old farmer wanted to know. I had. 'Then you have been *trespassing*.' He proceeded to give me a ten-minute harangue about how he paid £1,000 a year for the shooting rights on the Yorkshire Water Authority's moors and how I had no right to trespass. (It was not the shooting season.) 'We've given you the Pennine Way, we've given you the Brontë Way,' he continued. 'What more do you want? How would you like it if I came and took photographs in your back yard?'

The Yorkshire Water Authority had been particularly bad about access to the moors around Haworth, but were finally beginning to yield to pressure when water was privatised in 1989, bringing potentially far worse problems (see p. 18). As to shooting, whatever one's own view of blood-sports, the general public is denied access to large areas of land so that just a few can enjoy them.

I personally am unable to comprehend how I could be accused of 'trespassing' on a moor. It really is beyond my understanding. I have walked freely on the Alps, in the Tuscan hills, in the Appennines, Norway, Denmark, Holland, and many other places. How can I be accused of trespassing, on a moor, all alone?

Now, the owners of some of the biggest grouse moors in the country, have formed the powerful and elitist Moorland Association whose main aim is to prevent walkers having 'the right to roam' on grouse moors. Much of this heather moorland is common land, and if the Moorland Association gets its way, walkers will be strictly confined to footpaths, feeling like prisoners. Should a walker have the temerity to step off the path to get a better view for a photograph, or examine a rock, or a stream, or a flower, he or she may get the same rough treatment as the photographer at Brassington in Derbyshire (see p. 99).

The Government promised, in its 1987 election manifesto, to 'legislate to safeguard common land on the basis of the Common Land Forum' – the Forum recommended a right of public access on foot to all common land. In spite of pressure from the Ramblers' Association and the Open Spaces Society this promise had not been honoured at the time of going to press.

In 1970 Ted Hughes mentioned that he would like, at some time, to write poems about the Calder Valley area, but would like the visual stimulus of photographs to start him off. I went up, my first experience of the north, quite unlike the home counties which were more or less all that I knew of Britain at that time. I arrived in the dark, amazed by the switchback roads, and in the morning there were the grey moors with their gritty walls. That was the real beginning of my getting to know this country, where I felt a foreigner.

For several years I explored and photographed the British landscape. I visited Scotland, and a part of my heart was lost there forever. My mother was an American MacLean from Sutherland, so that probably had something to do with my feelings of recognition and identification with the far north, though she died young and had

not told me much about her family there. I worked on a number of books, mostly walkers' books, apart from *Remains of Elmet* with Ted Hughes. In a sense these were celebrations of our extraordinarily beautiful landscape and light, and its mysterious and fascinating traces of man; although I did not avoid the occasional blot on the landscape, I did not look for them. But when I assembled a retrospective collection for my book *Land*, I realised that it would be difficult for me to avoid confronting the degradation threatening the countryside. There are no absolutes: there is virtually no landscape in Britain that has not been worked, affected by human use, and this is what particularly interests me. Wilderness areas in the USA and more recently in New Zealand have fewer resonances for me.

Buildings and developments which were reviled during the last century have become today's heritage, today's archaeology. How can we be sure that what we see as threat and what we revile today will not be tomorrow's heritage? Well, I *am* sure about some of them. For instance, although an early twentieth-century concrete blockhouse may fool us into regarding it as archaeology, as the Ministry of Defence would wish, there is no way we can feel this way about our present defence installations, with their deadly eternities of arsenals which neither the MoD nor anyone else in the world know how to dispose of in a way which is acceptable to the public. We have polluted rivers, seas, the air; we do not know whether we can reverse the pollution, but we can try; we do know that we cannot dispose of the nuclear power residues for generations to come, yet we cut and cheat research into wind and wave power to protect the nuclear lobby. Some of what we leave will not be heritage or archaeology but a deadly legacy: the radioactive waste we create today will remain dangerous for longer into the future than the time the pyramids have been standing – it will be dangerous for 240,000 years.

Marion Shoard, in her remarkable book, *This Land is our Land*, suggests that 87 per cent of the land is in private ownership. The other 13 per cent includes roads, railways, airports and power stations and so on. The Forestry Commission, the MoD and the National Trust are the largest landowners. With water having been privatised, the water companies' land is likely to be used by commercial developers, so that we may lose access (see p. 18). The Forestry Commission has been forced to sell off some of its lands, with more sales due by the end of the century (see p. 17), and access has not been protected.

For the 87 per cent of privately owned land, I can't do better than to quote Alan Howard, Vice-Chairman of the Ramblers' Association: 'The four things about the countryside we tend as a nation to accept without question: ownership of much by few; owners' rights to vandalise; owners' rights to exclusive enjoyment of what remains unvandalised; and owners' rights to receive billions of pounds in handouts from the taxpayer.'

In Sweden everyone has had, from time immemorial, the right to roam on foot across another person's uncultivated land – Allemansrätt 'the right of all men' – so long as no damage is caused to landowners' property or the flora and fauna. Other Scandinavian countries and Holland have recently made most open uncultivated land accessible to walkers. Landowners in Britain faint at the thought, and protest that the public would ruin their estates. Here, the public has as a rule had no stake in the countryside, but there have been several interesting instances where, given access, people have not wrecked the land (see p. 71). Proper care for the land and its wildlife can be enforced by law; access on foot is surely an issue whose time has finally come.

Over 100 years ago, Richard Jefferies wrote in *The Pageant of Summer*, apropos the Thames: 'As the river above all things is, and ought to be, a place of recreation, care must be particularly taken that . . . the enjoyment of the many be not interfered with. The rational pleasure of 999 people ought not to be checked because the last of the thousand acts as a blackguard.'

We require more legislation by the Government to create access on foot, and to bring it further into line with countries such as Sweden, Norway, Denmark and Holland. In Britain there is much less access than when I was young. I believe there are two reasons for this. One is that many of the farmers were tenant farmers, who were less possessive about their land than the large agribusiness landowners we have now, and operated on a smaller, more human scale;· the other is that many of the owners of large estates have adapted their stately homes and gardens, or developed theme parks or heritage industries which are heavily marketed, drawing huge numbers of paying visitors, so the rest of their land is even more firmly fenced off to prevent it being overrun by the crowds.

We live in an era of attractions which are mass-marketed, and people are extremely mobile, but there is also a rapidly growing number of people who seek, and have a right to, quiet recreation in the countryside, on foot. If 'the right of all men' on uncultivated land were established in the UK, with more footpaths through cultivated areas, the serious erosion of the areas we are crowded into would decrease.

Apart from the historical loss of land to the large landowners, we have lost our land in a number of other ways: farming, forestry, military use of land, nuclear power stations and, finally, mass-marketing of tourism which will close off yet more land, as it has at Stonehenge (see p. 54). Where there is beautiful landscape, predatory developers circle, instead of attempting to redevelop derelict industrial sites first.

I love to walk – when paths have not been ploughed out of existence or barricaded – through a farming landscape, but I cannot relate to a chemical prairie, or to factory complexes housing suffering and sometimes diseased animals; herbivores fed on infected remains of other animals; cows with Bovine spongiform encephalitis (BSE or 'mad cow disease'). This was played down by the Ministry of Agriculture, Fisheries and Food (MAFF), who appeared more concerned at the economic effects on farming than on the health of the consumer. The scrapie-like disease has passed from sheep to cattle, and now to zoo animals, so there is no reason to suppose that it could not pass to humans. Neurologists, vets and farmers have told how they were cutting out some meat products from their diets because of what they knew about scrapie (Radio Four, *Face the Facts*). Helen Grant, a retired neuropathologist has seen cases of human spongiform encephalitis and says: 'What is alarming is the Government's behaviour.' Many farmers would prefer not to feed their animals with the infected remains of other animals, but the contents of animal feed do not have to be declared.

Dairy cattle are being given the genetically engineered hormone, bovine somatotrophin (BST) to boost milk yields, and this is now in our milk supply whether we like it or not. Farmers who object are not allowed to keep their milk separate, so consumers have no choice. How do we know what it will do to us? We don't, because the Official Secrets Act prevents open discussion. Dr Richard Lacey, Professor of Microbiology at Leeds University, stated, however, that the Veterinary Products Committee referred the possible long-term dangers of BST milk to the Department of Health on 21 September 1989. It was Dr Lacey who drew attention to the transmission of salmonella in eggs, and to the rapidly increasing number of cases of listeria. MAFF has more readily protected the interests of food producers than those of either consumers or the landscape; it has continued to protect the interests of factory-farmed eggs by imposing the same salmonella inspection fee regardless of whether there are 25 hens or 2,500, so that now it is almost impossible to find real 'free-range' eggs, one of the many pleasures of a visit to the countryside. As for milk, well, I've more or less given that up too, until I am allowed to choose non-BST milk. Dr Lacey resigned from his post at the end of 1989. It is to be hoped that when eventually the Government gives in – as it must – to public pressure for a separate Ministry of Food, that somebody like him will be appointed there.

The character of the countryside depends on farmers. High guaranteed prices to farmers through the Common Agricultural Policy as implemented by MAFF have resulted in the degradation of our landscape, and the removal of our hedges; one mile per daylight hour in the first half of the 1980s, even after the direct subsidies for hedgerow removal were scrapped. Fuelled by high returns, farmers have become businessmen, not concerned with the long-term health

of the land, but fired by the prospect of quick returns. Pesticides are used with insufficient care for the dangers to the people who handle them, for the damage to the food, the soil, or the people near by, including walkers. Dogs have died after being exercised on poisoned grass. If dogs die, surely toddlers will be next since they also breathe low to the ground.

In early 1989, friends of mine – parents with two young children – were out walking near Banbury on a fine, still, Sunday afternoon. They were on a hedgeless tarmac road, and a few hundred yards away a farmer was spraying his land on both sides of the road. He didn't turn off his spray as he continually crossed and recrossed the road, so that the road the family was walking on was wet with spray, and there were large foamy lumps of it at the road's edges. They could see, smell and *feel* the spray, and as they could not avoid breathing it in, they gave up their Sunday afternoon walk. My friend said he could still smell the spray, weeks later.

Of the many environmental programmes I have watched on television in the last couple of years, one made me particularly angry. Mark Purdey, a Devon farmer with a pedigree Jersey herd of seventy cows took MAFF to the High Court in 1985, and won against MAFF's directive that farmers should use organo-phosphates to control warble fly in cattle, since he considered it a serious hazard to the producers and consumers of food. He claims that he was then frequently harassed by MAFF, who finally revoked his licence to sell milk early in 1988, saying that his herd was unclean. Purdey made a film for the BBC's *Open Space*; when he started making the film, MAFF suddenly restored his licence, but it was too late: Purdey had given up and sold his herd to France, and was living, with his family, in rented accommodation.

The film showed a number of people who claim to have been affected, some by being sprayed accidentally in their own gardens. One woman was on crutches. Purdey himself believes that the pesticides may be linked to increases in multiple sclerosis, motor neurone disease and Alzheimer's disease. (Since it is thought that BSE could also eventually lead to Alzheimer's, MAFF may have a lot to answer for if we all end up mad, like the cows.)

Sir Richard Body, Conservative MP, a farmer, Chairman of Consumer Watch and former Chairman of the Commons Select Committee on Agriculture, made comments throughout the film: 'Organo-phosphates evolved out of chemical warfare in the First World War, used then to kill human beings, and I think the evidence against them is very strong indeed, and I think it's more than time that we questioned whether we should go on using them.' The film claimed that MAFF relies mainly on tests done by the chemical companies which cannot be made public because of the Official Secrets Act. Why? Because of commercial competition between manufacturers. Mark Purdey says that farmers don't have time to investigate all possible side effects of the products they use; they come with the tag 'Ministry Approved'. 'How can farmers be expected to become instant biochemists?' Body: 'I don't think the Official Secrets Act should apply to the safety of pesticides – the Act was passed before the First World War to protect the British people from German spies – in fact it's now being used to protect civil servants and pesticide manufacturers *against* the British people.'

In the post-war climate in which I grew up, where rationing persisted for many years, there was much talk of 'feather-bedding' farmers, which seemed reasonable, since food, after water, is *the* basic necessity. I believe this blinded a whole generation of us to what was actually happening. It is only in the last few years that I have realised the extent of the degradation of the landscape and of our food supplies. The two are inseparable.

In Lincolnshire, gangs are bussed in from midland cities to work the fields; they are often paid less than half the legal minimum rates of pay in cash only, by the 'gangmasters', who often fail to pass on their national insurance. If it's raining, they sit in the bus and don't get paid. If they complain, the bus doesn't pick them up next time. I spoke to a retired gangmaster: 'It will only be fair when all the workers are paid by cheque, too many are cheated in the present system.' A very few gangmasters have joined the Transport and General Workers' Union, but overall conditions are still poor. Lavatories are often not provided for the workers. 'As for the hygiene, after what I've seen, I wouldn't buy a strawberry in a shop, never ever ever.'

The quality of life and job satisfaction on this factory-farmed landscape are appalling, and some of the food may be rather less immaculate than it looks on the supermarket shelves.

The big farmers have benefited most from the high Common Agricultural Policy (CAP) subsidies and help from MAFF; their union, the powerful National Farmers' Union (NFU), represents the interests of the larger farmers better than those of the small farmers, who also have less time to attend meetings. Sir Richard Body stated in the *Independent* that altogether over the years, the NFU persuaded MAFF 'to provide farmers with forty different kinds of state aid, and, with one exception, they were each to the advantage of the large farmer and the comparative detriment of the small farmer.'

The large farmers swallowed up the small farmers, generously helped on by MAFF to produce expensive food mountains and milk lakes, and to poison the countryside with chemicals. MAFF, in the way it implements CAP, is no friend of the landscape. Having assisted the big farmers to pollute the countryside and our water supplies, the policies now subsidise them *not* to use nitrates in some areas. What other industry is paid *not* to pollute?

It is the small farmers who need generous subsidies to survive; they will never produce food mountains, but much of the character of the British countryside depends on them; the same applies to organic farmers, who have not polluted our soil or our water, or, equally important, our food; they have had no subsidies at all (see p. 170).

Apart from my passion for walking, I look to the countryside to provide the food I want to eat, and to produce untainted water. The Government is dismantling most of its food and agricultural research since it says that the manufacturers who benefit should do the research; but that way there is no official body to protect our interests as consumers. We are not allowed to see full test results on, for instance, irradiated food, or genetically altered yeasts; we are not given a choice. The Government is not accountable to the consumer. Most of the major nutritional research posts in our universities are funded by the food industry, which is not impartial; it will put its profits before our health. So we are left with one of the worst diets in Europe. When there are food scandals, as there have been in the last couple of years, MAFF protects the identities of the producers of contaminated food, and of sub-standard slaughter houses. Until we finally achieve freedom of information, we are shadow-boxing, though the ground swell of protest at our unreliable and often contaminated food is gathering momentum. Consumers should be allowed to exert 'market forces' to boycott sub-standard producers, and force them into better practice. Many of the problems are not the fault of farmers, but of farming policy. Philip Morgan, a farmer, recently wrote an article in the *Guardian*, from which I quote:

'Farming is a big business, not so much from the inclination of farmers, but because of the pressures of the support industries: the chemical industries that produce fertilizer, spray, antibiotics; the producers of machinery, tractors, harvesters, diggers, all of which are so heavy that they pulverise the soil and destroy the micro-life; the banks which lend the money to buy all these things; and the Government which bends the individual to its will . . .

'I hope that eventually people will see that the food we eat is hopelessly polluted, that our farming methods are killing the land,

and that profit is not the objective of tilling the soil. I hope that farming will be allowed by Government and business to become again a symbol of independence, and that farmers will be able to recognise that they are custodians of the future. If this happens, we can stop treating the land as an enemy. Then perhaps there will be a green spring to replace the blood-drenched, jack-booted apology for that season which characterises our farms today.'

In contrast, here is a quote from *Observer Scotland* from Ian Miller who began conversion to organic farming five years ago: 'It's been the toughest five years of my life,' he admitted. 'But never once did I think of going back to conventional farming. That would have been the easy option, because you can make a good living out of these 300 acres. But when I was using chemicals, I saw the heart go out of the land and that's what frightens me. What sort of legacy is that for your kids?'

Until recently I had supposed that only a few 'cranks' like myself would insist, wherever possible, on organic food, which is also far kinder to the land. I have a particular personal reason for preferring organic or biodynamic wholefoods. In 1976 I was very ill with advanced cancer. After good 'orthodox' treatment I was fortunate in being sent to the naturopath, Dr Gordon Latto, whose recommendation to eat as much fresh organically grown food as possible I adopted. I am certain it has helped my survival thus far. But there is a huge, unsatisfied demand for organic foods.

I wrote to Alan Gear, Chief Executive of the Henry Doubleday Foundation, founded by Lawrence D. Hills, and told him that I had always assumed that it would be impossible to feed the nation with organically grown food, and asked his opinion. He replied:
'I am totally convinced that organic farming is the only sustainable way of feeding the population. Chemical methods are leading to quite severe soil erosion in many places and are dependent upon high inputs of fertilizer and synthetic pesticides. These are oil-based and as we move into the twenty-first century are going to become increasingly expensive. If you couple this with the problems of residues of pesticides and nitrates in water supplies, plus the adverse effects on wildlife, you have a recipe for an untenable farming system. Organic farming on the other hand causes little or no pollution, and by recycling nutrients is much less dependent on outside inputs. So I would tend to rephrase the question: "For how much longer can we go on feeding ourselves by present chemical methods?"'

Alan Gear is, along with Jackie Gear and David Mabey, the author of *Thorson's Organic Consumer Guide*; and also one of the originators of the very popular TV series on organic gardening, *All Muck and Magic?* In his introduction to the guide – 'The Economics of Organic Farming' – Alan Gear writes about how organic growers are discriminated against because the plant breeders test new breeds with conventional (chemical) methods only: 'Research should be the

Government's responsibility, but UK plant variety breeding is being axed: the Plant Breeding Institute and the National Seeds Development Organisation were sold off to Unilever in 1988; the National Fruit Trials closed down in March 1990.'

In answer to the question, Is organic farming profitable? Alan Gear said: 'The farmer knows that even if the bottom drops out of the organic market and he has to sell his crop at conventional prices, he will be no worse off than if he had used chemicals.' He claims that the total cost of EEC support for agriculture in 1987 worked out at £11 a week for every British family. Add to this the cost of cleaning up our water supplies, polluted by chemicals, which will be borne by the consumer, and it makes the organic food look good value. 'As for pesticide pollution, there is no suggestion as to how this might be dealt with, let alone the cost.'

Spraydrift of chemicals not only pollutes the environment, it has caused a number of small organic growers to lose their symbols, with consequent serious loss of income. Surely it would be possible for the big agrochemical companies to have a compensation fund to deal with such unfortunate situations?

Marketing is one of the biggest problems as supermarkets demand that the produce be grown to exact sizes, and are unhelpful about delivery times. Organic farmers in west Wales have solved some of these problems by forming a successful co-operative. Otherwise most of the organic and biodynamic produce sold in supermarkets is imported. There is a growing and unsatisfied demand for organic and biodynamic food.

If we were to move on to organic farming, the countryside would be a far more pleasant and less dangerous place to be and to walk in.

Another danger is bulls. It is scandalous that they are allowed in fields where there are public footpaths. Every farmer I have ever spoken to has agreed that you can never trust a bull. Alan Sillitoe, with whom I worked on *The Saxon Shore Way* had an alarming confrontation with a bull on the long-distance footpath there. Peter Melchett, a farmer, says: 'Sooner or later somebody is going to be killed or injured by a bull on a public footpath – in my view it is inevitable.'

And then there are dogs. Ramblers are often confronted by a farmer with dogs on a public footpath, sometimes very aggressively. A rambler whose dog goes out of control in a field of sheep or cows can be fined and the dog shot, whereas if a farmer's dog attacks a rambler, the magistrate may order the farmer to keep his dog under control, but there will be no fine for the first offence. So it is a

greater offence in law for a rambler's dog to attack a farmer's sheep than it is for a farmer's dog to attack a rambler. Landowners and their dogs have more legal rights than ramblers.

Complaints to the police about farmers' harassment with dogs on public rights of way have generally been given short shrift. Recently, however, the Avon and Somerset police cleared up a long-standing menace in Clevedon, where dogs had been denying access to a public footpath. Cyril Trenfield, footpath secretary for Avon RA, complained, and the police agreed to send someone to accompany him incognito. The dogs made a lot of noise and the farmer demanded to know why they were walking there. They pointed out that it was a public right of way and reminded him of the law. The farmer said the law was an ass and asked who bothered abiding by it anyway. The policeman revealed his identity and warned the farmer that the police would attempt to obtain an order for the destruction of the dogs if the harassment persisted and the public was discouraged from using the path.

Let's hope that other police forces will likewise take a more positive line on rights of way threatened by the rapidly increasing number of vicious dogs. I personally feel threatened by dogs when out walking and have been harassed by them in the countryside and in public parks in London. The Government *must* be persuaded to bring in compulsory registration and insurance for dogs.

Forestry closes off large areas of land from the public. The setting up of the Forestry Commission after the First World War has much in common with the beginnings of subsidised farming after the Second World War. The Commission was set up in 1919 when the timber industry was in a run-down state, and there had been serious shortages, partly caused by enemy submarine activities. The Commission took over the running of 70,000 acres of Crown woods and was given huge funds to purchase and plant up land as state forests, and also to assist local authorities and private landowners with grants for new planting and renewal of older forests. Steve Tompkins in *The Theft of the Hills* explains how so much of our countryside, particularly in Scotland, came to be ruined by conifer plantation. Conifer forestry in itself has never been profitable, especially in the far north of Scotland, yielding a rate of return of only between 1 and 3 per cent, but the large grants and tax advantages for new planting of conifers and untaxed capital gains made the industry attractive to investors. In fact they were getting large areas of land for virtually no outlay. On small plantings of less than 2 acres, the grants in 1986 were about £255 per acre, and about £100 per acre on schemes over 25 acres. Typical schemes cover 400 to 3,000 acres. This has pushed up land prices, which were often as little as £10 per acre in Scotland, so that some of the most beautiful landscapes in the country have been obliterated by sterile and monotonous black conifers. The Forestry Commission is now the largest landowner in the UK. Taxpayers have paid for these massive grants and tax breaks for forestry.

When I spoke to Roger Bradley, the Commission's spokesman in Edinburgh, deploring the ruination of so much of the uplands, he claimed that of course the mistakes the Commission had made in the past had taken twenty or thirty years to show up, but that it now prides itself on careful landscaping of the forests and strict controls for private forestry. Unfortunately the controls are not always adhered to. For instance, a young forester friend of mine, who worked for a commercial forestry company in Scotland, told me that all contouring advice was ignored, that they planted in 'pin stripes' (alternate larch and spruce, rather than the attractive groupings the Commission had shown me in their plans), there was no regard for erosion, and the only concern was how many trees had been planted each day. He was so disgusted at the damage they were doing that he gave up the work.

The commercial forestry companies have not always shown concern for the countryside and communities where they operate. Friends near Lairg in the far north of Scotland told me that when large-scale conifer planting was proposed in their area, the local residents asked the company to give a formal undertaking that they would not use pesticides or herbicides since the chemicals would drain into the loch which provided their drinking water. The company refused to give any such undertaking.

Some of the companies do create some 'public relations' access – a visitor centre with perhaps a nature trail, but the land is in general not accessible to the public.

The Forestry Commission itself has steadily improved access to its lands and has made attractive and much publicised walks, with both car parks and visitor centres well planned and landscaped. Roger Bradley told me that the FC had found that more public access *reduced* fire risks and other damage – the public acted as unpaid wardens. However, the Commission has been forced by the Thatcher Government to sell off some of its lands, and when it has done so, it has not protected the access. When pressed as to why the Commission could not dedicate public rights of way, picnic sites and so on before they sell off the forests, Bradley replied that it might (or might not, the Commission didn't actually know) reduce the value of the land, and could infringe the 'privacy' of the landowner. I enquired whether they had ever tried it, and was told 'No – the moment you try it, you set a precedent.' Talk of being 'accountable' to the taxpayers sounded hollow on two counts: firstly, we, the taxpayers, have paid massively towards forestry, an unprofitable and environmentally damaging industry, and should expect some protected access in return; and secondly, since the Commission is not even certain that protecting some public access *would* reduce the value of the land, why not take a risk and try it? After all, the Government on our behalf has accepted heavy losses on sales to the private sector of Rover, the water authorities and other industries. The *only* conclusion is that public access to the countryside is a very low priority with the Thatcher Government.

Pen Wood on the Somerset–Dorset border is an example of the Forestry Commission selling some of its land to a private company, in this case the Unigate Pension Fund. The Ordnance Survey Landranger maps show it as having a car park and picnic site, and there was public access along tracks through the wood. When it was purchased by Unigate, the management was given to Forestry Investment Management Ltd, one of the big commercial forestry companies, which blocked off all public access. There has been so much adverse publicity that Unigate has now sold Pen Wood, but there is still no public access.

There have always been claims that forestry brings jobs, but there are not many, and, as analysed by Marion Shoard in *This Land is our Land*, each job created costs the public a staggering £238,000, while jobs created by the Highlands and Islands Development Board cost under £5,000. As the wild open country is enclosed and ruined by forestry, tourism will decrease and many more jobs will be lost than are created by it. Traditional ways of life are destroyed, and wildlife habitats are destroyed, many permanently. Unfortunately, far from being slowed down by the 1988 tax changes, which removed tax breaks from individual investors, the grants are simply being given out directly to commercial forestry companies, and the pace of new planting is accelerating, especially in the remote and beautiful flow country in the far north of Scotland (see p. 134). Forestry is a con trick, investors grow rich at taxpayers' expense as the land values rise, presided over and administered by the Forestry Commission.

A small gleam of cheer is that since the introduction of the Farm Woodland Scheme in 1988, there have been more subsidies and encouragement for broad-leaf woods, the woods we would all love to walk in. But although 76 per cent of planting in the UK under this scheme is financed by the taxpayers, there is *no* provision for access.

A much bigger gleam: in a new venture, called the Community Forests Initiative, the Countryside Commission and the Forestry Commission are planning to create forests around many of our major cities. They also plan a large new forest for recreation in the English midlands. Some of these new forests will be on wasteland, others on surplus arable land where there has been little public access. The plans seem wholly admirable, and should have the effect of taking some of the pressure off the countryside and country roads at the weekends, especially if adequately served by local public transport.

Water privatisation is one of the biggest threats to access to the open countryside that we have had to face. The land which we, having paid our dues to the authorities, felt was public land, has now been sold off to private companies, who will see their responsibilities to their shareholders as far more important than the matter of public access. We are likely to see land being sold off for development, leisure schemes, time-shares and so on. In fact writs have been issued against eight of the ten water companies. As Clive Betts, Sheffield Council leader, said in November 1989, 'Legally and morally, the assets belong to our ratepayers, and any profits made from them should benefit all the community instead of a handful of individuals.'

In March 1989 Nicholas Ridley announced a new safeguard to 'protect the beauty and amenity of water industry land in the national parks after privatisation'. But it will do no such thing, since it requires the water industry only to 'take into account' views expressed by the national parks on 'significant action affecting landscape, conservation and land management' by the water industry in the parks. Worst of all, it will not enable national parks to prohibit inappropriate developments.

As well as posing a serious threat to landscapes in national parks, the Water Act threatens to ruin the enjoyment of millions of people who walk over land until recently owned by water authorities, including vast tracts of open country in the Peak District National Park, in the Pennines, the Lake District and Wales. Much of this open country – nearly half a million acres – mainly mountain and moorland, has been opened up after public pressure only in the recent past, having been out of bounds for decades. It is ironic that historically the water authorities denied access to the public because of 'pollution' risks, or even on the grounds that they might behave immorally, but they allowed fishermen on to their lands, no doubt assuming that they were more continent than the general public. A further irony is that lead weights, discarded or spilt by fishermen, were poisoning the swans in many areas – lead weights have now been banned.

However, it has become obvious that the real polluters were agriculture and sewage. There is a growing threat of deadly algae in many inland waters and reservoirs resulting from nitrogen and phosphates. Many recreation facilities are faced with closure, but the problem was played down with water privatisation looming. By spring 1990, even in the very few months following privatisation, it had become clear that the new water companies face colossal costs to reverse decades of neglect and pollution, and they are likely to look for new ways of making money out of what should remain open landscapes, accessible to all. The 1989 Water Act specifically allows the privatised water companies to levy a charge for public access.

The Government has created a new body, the National Rivers Authority, claiming that it will be an 'independent' watchdog to police the water authorities, but one day after privatisation we heard that the Government has curbed its powers, and the Authority has no control over pesticide pollution anyway. (Why not?) After all the public relations hype about an independent watchdog with teeth, are they in fact false? And are fines a sufficient deterrent, when farmers and industrialists simply regard fines as running costs, cheaper than

putting things right, or should we, like some states in the USA, be thinking in terms of criminal proceedings for pollution?

David Beskine, Countryside Officer of the Ramblers' Association, ran the campaign to save public access to water authority land after privatisation. He writes:

'When the Government first mooted water privatisation, not a word was said about retaining the "right to roam" over almost half a million acres of wonderful, unspoilt mountainous countryside. The Government perhaps hoped that nobody would notice that by privatising this undeveloped land with no safeguard for public access, a huge potential windfall would come the way of investors. But public reaction to the loss of what is akin to a basic civil liberty – the simple freedom to walk unmolested across vast swathes of water-gathering ground – confirmed what we long believed: there is a huge demand for *greater* freedom of access to our countryside, as well as protecting what we already enjoy.

'Although we forced the Government to make some amendments as privatisation went through Parliament, in reality the private companies' hands have not been tied. North West Water, for example, has advertised for a manager to be responsible for the commercial development of its landholdings.

'We did manage to get 20 per cent of water authority land firmly protected in law, but that leaves the remaining 80 per cent exposed to predatory market forces. Apart from the Government retaining a theoretical power to intervene when land is sold, the only constraint imposed on the new private landowners is fourteen weasel words of barely any value: the Water Act states that the water undertakers (but not their subsidiaries or any subsequent landowners) must "have regard to the desirability of preserving for the public any freedom of access". There is no firm duty to protect access – all they need do is think about it, "have regard" to it, then presumably forget about it for ever. But we in the RA, and many others, will not let the water companies forget about access: water privatisation was a recipe for conflict, much of which has yet to occur.'

On the subject of conflict, all over Britain there are military exclusion areas – the MoD is the second largest landowner in the country. The military demand for land is insatiable, with no apparent spending restraints – in spite of glasnost it is acquiring 50,000 acres more. It emphasises that it buys the land on the open market, that it is not compulsorily purchased, but with its spending power this is not difficult. Just as well since its record on temporary requisitions during the Second World War is a bit tarnished: take Greenham Common (see p. 55), Tyneham (see p. 81) and six villages in the Stanford Training Area (see p. 77), for example. During the war people were prepared to make sacrifices, but they expected the military to keep its promise to return their land after the war. Fifty years later all is still in military hands. In the early 1980s it acquired 600 acres of Luddesdown, an extremely beautiful green-belt area just outside London with many conservation designations. When I visited the area which has some of the best-kept paths I have seen, I was amazed that the MoD could even think it possible to use such exquisite, well used landscape for military training, just where there was enormous pressure from London and nearby areas. Fortunately the residents from this affluent area were able to fight it off with a widely publicised campaign.

The money the MoD is making from disposals (surplus land – not training areas in the countryside) is enormous: £640 million since 1979; the MoD is expecting a further £500 million between 1990 and 1995. I don't suppose, however, that it contributed any of these profits to compensate the residents who had to find large sums to stop the MoD using Luddesdown or similar areas for training.

The military purchased Holcombe Moor, north of Manchester, a large area of common land with a right of public access. There has been a tough campaign, led by the Ramblers' Association, to prevent the MoD from converting it into a training area. Although the military did not propose to extinguish access, it simply forgot or overlooked the fact that there is an inalienable right of access and that the moor is thus unsuitable for military training. When RA pointed out the error, the MoD refused to give way, and has consistently been pushing for something quite outrageous – mass military training with up to 650 men at a time on public access land! At the time of going to press the outcome of the public inquiry into this proposal has yet to come.

The MoD tried to acquire one of the last great wilderness areas in Scotland, a mountain wilderness called Knoydart. Fortunately it withdrew, and 3,000 acres of this land were bought by the newly formed John Muir Trust, whose aim is 'to conserve and protect wild land for future generations, while respecting the needs and aspirations of those living in such areas'.

At times the military seems to feel that it is above the law, as when it simply stopped the public using rights of way at Lydd (see p. 74). In spite of its huge resources and colossal overspending, the military does not feel it has a responsibility to remove the hideous messes it has made in the landscape, such as those on the Hebridean shores (see p. 156); it does not even always remove dangerous materials before letting the public back on to the land (see p. 76).

Of course we need an army, but I am one of many who are totally opposed to nuclear defence. Not only does it impoverish the country and deprive the education and social services of badly needed funds, it is also stockpiling a deadly legacy of which we do not know how to dispose. I believe the battles of the coming generations will have more to do with environmental problems than with frontiers and military defence. If those deadly arsenals were to be used there would be nothing left to defend.

I went to visit Faslane, home of Trident, and had a long conversation with Ivy Sutherland, teacher and secretary of the local amenities society. I asked her how the military had acquired so much land in Coulport's nuclear triangle – Coulport, Faslane and Holy Loch – without compulsory purchase:

'It's an insidious thing. They establish a base; they then make life so uncomfortable for the people round about them, that the people sell and get out, so the military expand by buying their property.

'Another thing that has really annoyed local people is all these notices that have sprung up like mushrooms – "MoD Property" – and they actually planted one of these in the garden of a doctor friend of mine in Garelochhead!

'The MoD now say that they need to blast away large lumps of the shingle strand that juts out into the Gare loch, at the mouth of the loch, in order to get the Trident submarines in and out, so the people are wondering what is going to happen to the tides, what's going to happen to their shore . . .'

I too experienced the heavy-handed military presence. Since I did not want to get arrested, I wrote and was given permission to photograph the perimeter fence from the public road (see p. 59). When I arrived, letter in hand, I took the added precaution of reporting in to the main gate, explaining what I was doing, and expressing the hope that I would not be arrested. 'It's fine, we'll let everyone know. Go ahead,' the Duty Officer said pleasantly. I did not spend very long there, about half an hour – the atmosphere was horrible. Just as I was walking back to my car, a MoD vehicle abruptly pulled up, and a policeman stopped me, and peremptorily demanded to know what I was doing. I explained, and produced the letter. The policeman insisted that I should tell him who I was working for, and had difficulty in understanding that I was working for myself. Every line of the letter was noted, and he followed me back to my car to take the details. All this was on a public road. I would *hate* to live there.

There has been a lot of conflict over Greenham Common. Sixteen out of 96 missiles were removed on 1 August 1989 as agreed in the

US-Soviet INF (intermediate-range nuclear forces) treaty of 1987, but 'we've nothing to celebrate until the entire base is shut and restored as common land,' said a Greenham peace campaigner. Here is a letter from Richard Adams, published in *The Times* on 14 November 1989:

'Sir, During my childhood, before the Second World War, Greenham Common was a superb public open space; a great, heathery waste forming the watershed between the Kennet and the Enborne brook (which runs into the Kennet at Aldermaston). It was covered with expanses of 'real' bell heather (*Ardea cinerea*), while unusual wild flowers, such as droseraceae (catch flies) were also to be found in wetter places.

'The natural wild life was exciting: it included three kinds of snake, one or two kinds of lizard, stoats, weasels, rabbits and stag beetles, together with several different kinds of grasshopper and ant. The public had access to all this, and I myself spent many happy hours there. It is about three miles from Newbury to Brimpton (where the Common ended) and about a mile across from the Kennet to the Enborne.

'In 1941 the Common was taken by the Ministry of Defence for an airfield. There was little opposition. Hitler was on the doorstep and people were ready to make almost any sacrifice that would help

England, standing alone against Germany. After the war, however, the MoD retained the Common because they wanted it for a nuclear air base. This was the time of the Cold War so that again there was not a great deal of local opposition.

'Now, Greenham Common has ceased to be a nuclear air base and the missiles are all going, so we are told. But the Ministry of Defence intend to retain the air base for reasons that they have never really divulged. The case is fully as unjustifiable as that of Crichel Down in the 1950s.

'The department say they are going to buy out commoners' rights at £700 per commoner (there aren't a great many people who are actually "commoners" within the meaning of the law). But why should Newburians and other local people be deprived of this public open space, just because it is nearly 50 years since it was taken away?

'With one mouth the Government are emphasising the importance of public open space and of the 'green' cause, while with the other they are saying that for undisclosed reasons they don't mean to give back Greenham Common or restore it to what it used to be. To me and a great many other people, this makes no sort of sense at all – except a sense of injustice.'

I wonder if in the future our enormous military resources, and their great reservoirs of talent, training and intelligence, might be deployed in reversing the damage we have allowed to our environment? Let us hope, at least, that they will be more accountable to the public about their voracious appetite for land, and that we can stop feeling that we need to defend our land *from* the military, who state: 'The Defence of the realm will override all other considerations,' MoD Annual Report, 1984.

Nuclear power has aroused progressively more hostility with the public, especially since Chernobyl when vast areas, even as far away as Britain, were so badly contaminated that in many places, four years later, sheep are still too radioactive to take to market. What happens to people in these areas?

I have visited Dungeness (see p. 61) over a long period, and have spent time photographing people on the beach with the reactors breathing down their necks.

'The history of the project is one of astonishing chaos and incompetence,' wrote Richard Ingrams in 1979. 'Even the CEGB now admits to "straight-forward engineering idiocy" ' (from Ingrams' and my book, *Romney Marsh*). Ten years on things are even worse. Although construction of Dungeness B started in 1965, the second reactor there was not connected to the national grid until 1985, by which time it was a local joke that Dungeness was the safest nuclear power station to work in, since the only deaths were from old age. Dungeness B is now referred to as one of the 'basket cases' by nuclear experts and the industry – along with two other advanced gas-cooled reactors (AGRs). Greenpeace/Friends of the Earth figures show that during the twelve months to May 1989, the reactor only produced 11.8 per cent of its projected capacity. The AGRs perform less well than the antiquated Magnox stations they are replacing. It would be cheaper to decommission the accident-prone Dungeness reactor than to try and continue working with it. But nobody knows how to decommission it or how much it will cost, since no other country has built AGRs.

Dungeness B has cost the taxpayer five times more than estimated. It's ironic that the nuclear power lobby's promises of cheap and clean nuclear electricity were seen to be fraudulent by a notable own goal when city accountants looked into the books during preliminary discussions about privatisation. In 1989 there was a historic, because first, prosecution of the CEGB for two accidents at Dungeness which had resulted in workers trying to 'hoover' up shattered fuel assembly rods. The fine was £3,000, derisory damages, since the cost of the accidents will run into millions and no doubt the taxpayer pays the fine anyhow. The QC defending said: 'Its *exemplary* record was now tainted' (my italics). Local residents are sceptical about claims that there was no danger from these accidents and there were two serious radioactive leaks from the geriatric Magnox Dungeness A during 1987–8.

The fine wilderness area of Dungeness, with its unique shingle banks, is the largest of its kind in Europe and possibly in the world. Once crossed only by footpaths and by birds on the wing, much of it is now enclosed and a right of way extinguished. The squat blocks dominate the beach, high-voltage pylons march across the shingle, killing swans and other birds from the bird reserve near by. Dungeness, with its rare flora, is an SSSI, and was one of the last habitats of the little tern on the south coast. It is proposed as a Ramsar site (an internationally designated wetland site), a special protection area, and most recently as a National Nature Reserve. But the invaluable wilderness has been lost, wasted, along with the billions squandered on radioactive waste.

One of the biggest threats to the countryside is our transport policy, or rather lack of it. Many of us have to use cars for our work, for shopping and taking children to school; but often we have to use cars because of the lack of suitable public transport. The Government's policy that public transport must be made to pay for itself is the opposite of that in many European countries, where it is heavily subsidised.

It is virtually impossible to live in the countryside without a car now since there are so few buses. The latest disaster is the poll tax which will close down many of the village shops which have so far managed to survive. With them will probably go village post offices, and that will finally make it impossible for people without a car to live in villages. This particularly affects older people who are no longer able to drive.

The Government has announced that it is doubling spending on road-building during the next ten years, and yet it proclaims it is 'green'. Cars are the single biggest polluter; they rob us of land: each mile of motorway takes 25 acres of land, and who knows how much devastation from quarrying. They also pollute what is left of the countryside with tourism.

We are all tourists some of the time. Where I totally disagree with what is happening is the way we are marketing our heritage and landscape to death. Just look at Stonehenge! It was left to the nation by private owners under the following conditions, among others:

a) The public to have free access to the monument, on payment not exceeding 1/- per head per visit, subject to whatever conditions the Department (of the Environment – now cared for by English Heritage) may impose;
b) That the monument shall be kept as far as possible in its condition in 1918.

Unfortunately the pressures of tourism, followed by vigorous advertising by English Heritage, have made these two conditions incompatible. If there is free access, the monument will be ruined. English Heritage state: '. . . if permitted to wander freely among the stones, large numbers of visitors would slowly, but surely, erode and damage the monument itself, simply by touching or standing on the fallen stones. This is one area where our duty to preserve a monument conflicts with our desire to display it to the public. When this occurs, we take the view that preservation must come first.'

I cannot believe that a system of limited access to the stones would be impossible, perhaps admitting the first hundred people a day, or a week, or a year. Something must be possible. In fact English Heritage did have a system of one-day-a-week winter access until 1986, and say that though 'no significant damage was caused, certain areas became worn'. I spoke to a senior county archaeologist who also felt that limited access must be possible.

In the past, photographers have had access to the stones, and with each generation there have been personal interpretations of Stonehenge by artists such as Bill Brandt, Paul Caponigro, and others, who have spent time with the stones and got to know them. But when I wrote a very polite letter to English Heritage, complete with curriculum vitae, requesting a pass to take photographs over a period of time, outside normal visiting hours, I was told that I would have to cope with film crews making advertisements (which I was quite prepared to do) and that I would also have to pay a fee of £200 *per visit*. Though advertising groups can afford to pay huge location fees, I do not expect to be charged for creative work, nor could I afford such fees anyway. Eventually, after a protest to the Director of English Heritage the fee was magnanimously waived, but with the request that I only went once because of 'administrative problems'. There have been so many fine interpretations of Stonehenge over the years that it would be unthinkable for me to attempt *in one visit* the kind of pictures I would like to have taken; much time is needed to find one's personal view of a much-photographed monument. From now on, the only photographs we are likely to see of the inner circles of Stonehenge will be those *approved* by English Heritage, generally by their anonymous public relations photographers.

The problems of Stonehenge will not go away. Stonehenge is central to our culture, and just bringing in large numbers of police to stop people attending the solstices will not solve things. I was there for the summer 1988 solstice. There was a very nasty atmosphere. I took a snap with a small amateur camera and as it was still dark the flash went off. A policeman turned round and said: 'If you take any more pictures I'll smash your camera.' This was *before* the riots started. Although the 'hippies' undoubtedly started these particular riots, the police seemed to be spoiling for a confrontation.

Surely a space could be found for the 'hippies' to camp legally, perhaps on some of those miles of MoD land at Larkhill, near the proposed Visitor Centre, and a fee could be charged to cover the cost of cleaning up the garbage, as has happened at the Glastonbury Festival. Cars would not be permitted within an appropriate radius of Stonehenge, and many of the revellers would no doubt stay at the camp with their festival and drinks and so on, and those who really wanted to go to the solstice would have to walk. There is a race-course on MoD land at Larkhill maintained at taxpayers' expense which might provide an admirable site for such a temporary camp . . .

Nearly 700,000 people visit Stonehenge each year, largely as a result of advertising. Surely it is not too much to ask that English Heritage find a solution to the solstice problems, and that they make some provision for photographers and artists to have occasional access? If not, we shall continue to feel that English Heritage have robbed us of our heritage.

Mass-marketing of our heritage and landscape leads to more and more pressure on the roads as there is seldom adequate public transport. We are lured into the countryside, only to find most of it out of bounds, while we are fobbed off with substitutes like country parks and theme parks. As pressure on the countryside has grown, the Government has paid lip-service to the idea of nature conservation by designating SSSIs. Roads have already damaged 110 SSSIs, however, and Friends of the Earth figures show that 155 more are under threat in England, with the latest road-building plans.

The Department of Transport is so dedicated to the car that it ignores the needs of cyclists, whether they are commuting to work in the cities, or cycling in the countryside for recreation. They don't pollute, but are maimed or killed, since they are not taken into account in planning. Some apologetic little tracks have recently appeared in Camden in London, where I live, but I find them nearly as dangerous as the road as they seem to be designed for cramped single-file cycling, and peter out just where they are most needed. At least they are newly surfaced though, giving a brief respite from the back-breaking pot-holes all over the Camden roads.

Apart from the danger of accidents, the fumes emitted by Government transport policy are poisonous; in London, where I have cycled for well over thirty years, street-level ozone is often well above World Health Organisation maximum recommended levels, and can cause all sorts of illnesses and allergies. Mrs Thatcher claims that Britain is taking a lead in reducing the greenhouse effect and pollution, but with our present transport policies we will continue to increase pollution and emissions of greenhouse gases in and from the UK.

Roads have destroyed many of our towns and cities, and they destroy the countryside. The environmentally damaging implications of placing the Channel Tunnel terminal near the white cliffs of Dover (see p. 121) rather than further north around Ashford or Redhill have yet to be understood by much of the public; lorry traffic is set to double, and there will be an enormous influx of motorists from the Continent.

If the Government is serious about its 'green' credentials, it will have to have a radical rethink about its transport policies. It will need to show proper concern about the destruction of our countryside and

cities by 'the great car economy', and recognise that pedestrians and cyclists have a right to move around without risking life and limb. It will have to stop motor traffic from using 'green lanes', the only remaining unsurfaced 'roads' in Britain, in very much the same state as when horse and cart were last driven along them (until, that is, the free-wheeling motor-cyclists and four-wheeled drive fanatics churn them up, wrecking the lanes for others in the name of fun). There have been vigorous campaigns for years to restrict motor traffic from the Ridgeway, our oldest prehistoric trackway. Even the AA, not usually in favour of restricting motor traffic, has called for the right of way to 'these old, unsurfaced cross-country tracks to be restricted to walkers, cyclists, horseriders and agricultural vehicles'!

As Andrew Lees of Friends of the Earth said recently, there is no such thing as a 'green' car. Not only does it pollute on the road, it is a major cause of pollution in manufacture. Volvo have recently taken voluntary steps to clean up their production line with environmental technology; they have invented a way of recycling CFCs and their new paint shop will be solvent-free; their intention is that all air and water leaving the factory should be clean. Surely it is time that some of *our* chemical and industrial giants became more heavily involved in such technology? And in making repairable goods with long guarantees instead of the goods with a built-in throw-away factor we are now sold . . . There must be money in it too.

There are, of course, other sorts of pollution. One of the worst problems has been toxic waste disposal and our cavalier attitude towards it. There are at present no controls as to who runs waste tips; much of the waste in them is unidentified and can be a major hazard to water supplies, as well as to people. Methane gas is also a regular danger (see pp. 46 and 109). Many sites are unmanned and unfenced, so children get on to them; there are public footpaths going right through the middle of some tips. A House of Commons Welsh Affairs Committee Report, in March 1990, called for much stricter regulations, fencing and monitoring, and for footpaths to be diverted (rather than extinguished altogether, as some local authorities favour).

We not only fail to dispose of our waste, we have a rapidly growing industry in disposing of other countries' waste, often with very few controls. It is a very lucrative industry, and residents and newspapers have been involved in serious libel actions after opposing specific proposals. It is a scandal to import toxic waste when we can't even dispose of our own.

We should bring in legislation and taxes to encourage clean production in industry – so we don't produce toxic waste in the first place.

Our 140,000 miles of footpaths in England and Wales are unique, in that they derive from ancient rights of way, and the fact that they are as much a part of the Queen's Highway as are tarmac roads. In other countries large networks of footpaths have been created specifically for walks. This is so in the Alps, in France, in Australia and New Zealand. I visited New Zealand recently, where there is an impressive network of well maintained paths in wilderness and conservation areas, but virtually none through farmed landscape. One of the delights of walking in Britain used to be to walk through farmed landscape. That is, until agribusiness set in.

Governments have done little to increase public access to open country on foot, though in the brave new world after the Second World War, The National Parks and Access to the Countryside Act 1949 did make an attempt. The Act defines 'open country' in England and Wales as 'mountain, moor, heath, commons, down, cliff or foreshore'. The Countryside Act 1968 extended this to include woodlands, rivers, canals and the banks of rivers and canals. But neither Act actually gave us a *right* of access!

Every bit of access had to be separately negotiated, with suitable compensation, with landowners, but not many access agreements were obtained. Most of those were in the Peak District, and it seems that some of them may be in jeopardy when they come up for renewal in the early 1990s. Since there were so few agreements, pressure on the space was heavy; if we had overall access, the pressures of erosion and public use on the limited spaces would be reduced.

The 1949 Act stipulated that local authorities draw up a 'definitive' map of footpaths. In the main, the authorities asked parishes to supply information for the maps. Some were careless, and others were in the power of the large landowners who were not necessarily inclined to ensure that all rights of way were put on the 'definitive maps'. In one area the local RA group estimates that only 10 per cent of such paths were marked through a large estate. So that the Act, intended to promote access, in some cases actually led to footpaths being reduced. However, those paths which did find their way on to the definitive map were given some form of permanent protection; once on the map, they were legally recognised and no matter what a landowner gets up to, he or she cannot get rid of the path except through a legal process.

The 1949 Act led to the creation of the National Parks. Ours are quite different from those in many other countries, which are often mainly State-owned wilderness areas. In England and Wales the land in the parks is privately owned, but the National Park status protects the landscapes, which is admirable in theory. The upland farms in many of our national parks make up some of the most attractive and characteristic countryside we have; unfortunately EEC policies have been much less supportive to small farmers, many of whom are finding it a struggle to survive. Other areas of national parks have been spoiled by agribusiness – the protective status did not protect against changes in farming methods, nor against blanket conifer afforestation. The countryside is beautiful, but whole hillsides are being quarried away to build more roads to more tourist complexes for more tourists. During the last ten years or so there has been an explosion in tourist development in or on the fringes of national parks. Local authorities who have tried to stop inappropriate developments have had their decisions overturned by the Government; they then have less control over the developments than if they had given the go-ahead in the first place.

Developers and speculators are being allowed to swamp many of our national parks, cheered on by our transport policies for more roads and more cars. Saturation marketing takes place to get enough people to fill the tourist complexes – not only marketing the development but the particular area as well. In 1989 several National Park areas took the unprecedented step of putting embargoes on advertising or even mentioning certain over-used areas in tourist literature. No wonder some Scottish rangers and others are ambivalent towards suggestions that national parks should be introduced north of the border. 'Look what's happened to yours,' they say. People living in national parks find they are still not protected against major tourist, quarrying or other developments; but petty bureaucracy is rampant when it comes to changing the sizes of windows, allowing signs for B & Bs or cafés.

In New Zealand people were stunned when I described our own national parks. No pesticides are used in theirs, there is no quarrying, and in most cases no visitors' dogs. In addition to the national parks, they have many other types of conservation area. Of course in New Zealand they have huge tracts of land, which we do not. The original idea of our national parks was fine; it is greed which is wrecking them, whether in the form of tourist developments, business interests or sheer folly. For instance, the CEGB had a massive advertising campaign to show how green and environment-friendly they are, in the run-up to privatisation. They showed how they had buried a huge power station inside Ilidir Fawr, just north of Snowdon, producing 1,800 megawatts. They did not however show pictures of the pipelines from the 10-megawatt station, a massive eyesore at Cwm Dyli on the flanks of Snowdon which is, according to legend, the last resting place of King Arthur's sword Excalibur. This station provides enough power for all of 3,000 domestic storage heaters. Despite local and national protest, the CEGB went ahead. Chris Brasher wrote an extremely moving article in the *Observer*, describing 'Marshall's Folly' as 'a memorial to the way we rape this earth'.

One final indicator of 'the great car economy': while roads are pushed through SSSIs and national parks with barely an apology, many of our public footpaths even in national parks and National Trust areas are blocked. To avoid over-use and erosion, we need more paths, not less. Highway authorities' expenditure on roads is colossal. It would take a fraction to put the footpaths in order. But it *would* take the will.

The third largest landowner in Britain is the National Trust, which owns land on behalf of all of us. As well as its much-publicised stately homes, it owns large tracts of land and coast. By and large its record is impressive, with sensitive and appropriate handling of the open countryside areas, though with an organisation as large as the Trust there are of course criticisms. One is that although it owns land on behalf of all of us, it tends to be too 'landownerish' and complacent at times. Many of us who delight in photographing its gardens have been tapped on the shoulder by wardens wanting us to pay a 'facility fee', though Head Office categorically states that this is not National Trust policy. Let's hope it filters through to the regions.

There have been problems at Milldale in the Peak District (see p. 87), as with Patrick Heron's land (see p. 94). Even the 'inalienable' tag has been known to slip as in the unfortunate saga of Bradenham Bunker in 1981. This caused such an outcry among its huge membership (currently 1.8 million) that a group calling itself the National Trust's Countryside Protection Group was set up within the Trust to try to reflect grass-root opinion, and to keep the executives in touch with their membership.

When one considers the reasonable balance of access, conservation and car parks in most National Trust areas, one must be thankful that it is there. What a tragedy that it was unable to purchase Land's End – its plans were so much more imaginative and appropriate than Peter de Savary's (see p. 92). It is difficult to understand why the Trust was not helped with central Government funds since money does exist for such purchase through the National Heritage Memorial Fund.

Other smaller landowners have emerged in the last few years who own land on behalf of the public. The Woodland Trust has grown extremely rapidly since the early 1970s, and already has a membership of over 65,000. It owns more than 400 woods across 56 counties in England, Scotland and Wales, covering over 12,500 acres. Its policy is one of open public access to its woods, which in many cases were previously closed to the public.

'From a wildlife conservation point of view, woods are robust habitats . . . The vast majority of visitors keep to paths and rides from choice; if necessary, routes can be directed away from extremely sensitive wildlife areas. We know that in many Trust woods wildlife abounds and even shy birds breed successfully year after year,' wrote Elizabeth Hamilton in the June/July 1988 issue of the *Rambler*. 'We also reap the produce of the woods by using traditional management techniques such as coppicing and selection systems. These have been practised for centuries in Britain without harm to the woodland environment.'

No wonder their membership has grown so dramatically. People love woods, but they often do not love forestry as practised in this country. In the USA and in Denmark massive public and political pressure has transformed the official forestry agencies. Conservation and recreation are now equal in importance to timber production. State forestry is now being expanded in both countries, rather than being sold off to the private sector as it is here. Perhaps we could start lobbying for more sympathetic handling of forestry in this country; much of the hostility we feel for present forestry methods could be defused if the forestry lobby changed its approach. Let's hope that the Community Forests Initiative signals the beginning of change (see p. 18).

A newcomer to this area of holding land on behalf of the public is the recently formed John Muir Trust (see p. 20).

There are many environmental organisations: Greenpeace, Friends of the Earth, the Council for the Protection of Rural England; the bodies which specifically campaign for access to open country are the Ramblers' Association, and the smaller Open Spaces Society. The Ramblers' Association campaigns for our inalienable right to use our public footpaths, our right to roam in open country, and to defend the natural beauty of the countryside, as well as promoting rambling. The ramblers' movement began with workers and their families needing to get out of the furnace cities of the industrial revolution, to get back to their roots in the countryside which they had so recently left, but which had been enclosed in the mean time. Many of the early ramblers were naturalists and fine conservationists; but even in those days landowners and their servants and gamekeepers were determined to keep them out. 'The importance of land to the power holders in British society is difficult to over-estimate,' wrote Tom Stephenson in *Forbidden Land*.

The present Government has introduced one welcome reform regarding access to the countryside: landowners who open their estates up to the public are granted exemption from Inheritance Tax. This is admirable in principle, but there is a catch – the Treasury refuses to publish details of what land has been made available on the basis that all tax matters are strictly confidential! The RA is pressing hard for the public to be told what public access has been achieved by tax exemptions.

The first Federation of Rambling Clubs was formed in 1905, and the Ramblers' Association proper in 1935. From small beginnings, membership has grown to nearly 80,000, with an additional 76,000 affiliated members. It is a truly democratic association, and its strength lies in its formidable and effective lobbying power both at national and local levels. From its small London headquarters nation-wide campaigns are conducted, most notably in recent years the Forbidden Britain Campaign. The RA has over 330 local groups, which look after local paths, produce guide books and organise walks, and when necessary lobby local authorities about blocked footpaths and similar problems. It has published a definitive legal textbook, *Rights of Way: A Guide to Law and Practice*, and has built up such a reputation for expertise that many people think it is the official custodian of footpaths, although it is a voluntary organisation and depends on its membership for funding.

The RA ran a vigorous campaign to save public access to water authority land after privatisation (see p. 18). It has run campaigns against the removal of hedgerows, against pesticides on rights of way, for the removal of tax exemptions on conifer afforestation, and it played a crucial role in the creation of national parks. Its 1990 major campaign – 'Head for the Hills, the right to roam' – coincided happily with a full-page feature in the *Guardian* (5 January 1990) called 'Forbidden Britain', which included articles by Tony Benn, by Richard Adams on the continued occupation of Greenham Common by the military, and by David Fairhall about access and, in particular, access to common lands. Clearly the importance of these issues is now being widely recognised.

The invitation to be President of the Ramblers' Association from 1987 to 1990 came as a complete surprise. Although I had been a member for over thirty years I had not been closely associated with it. But my work had of course been involved with walking and the countryside, and I had published several walkers' books. I regarded it as an honour, and it has been a privilege to hold the position for these last three years. I was aware of the contributions of my immediate predecessors, Mike Harding, Peter Melchett, and, of course, Tom Stephenson who was instrumental in persuading the Attlee Government to introduce the 1949 Act.

I felt that my own best contribution as President would be a book, and decided at the time to work on *Our forbidden land*, the title inspired by the Forbidden Britain campaign, and my earlier book, *Land*. In 1989 Tom Stephenson's book, *Forbidden Land*, the history of the struggle for access to mountain and moorland, was published. I tried to think of other titles for my book, but none would do. So I decided to stick to my title, and hope it will be seen as an act of homage to one of the great figures in the Ramblers' Association, and as a sharing of his aims.

Of course, for me, it had to be a book of photographs, but photographs can be ambiguous; normally I am happy to let people interpret my pictures in their own way, but I decided that for this book the ambiguities should be clarified whereas on the wall I will leave it to the viewer. I intended my book to be an exploration of access, but once I started, the question of what sort of countryside we were asking for access *to* could not be avoided. So it has become my personal exploration of the environment now.

We are forbidden access to our land in more ways than the strictly physical one. There are many places we are not allowed to photograph (see pp. 10 and 99), the royal parks, Stonehenge and many monuments and museums. It is illegal for instance to set up a tripod in Trafalgar Square.

Photographer Rolf Richardson described recently in the *British Journal of Photography* how he was forbidden to take pictures in the piazza at Covent Garden, but had no trouble setting up his tripod in NASA Mission Control! The British restrictions on 'professional' photography amount to a form of censorship; in time we might only see 'approved' pictures of some of our monuments and gardens. There is a wonderful story about Ansel Adams being tapped on the shoulder after he had set up his tripod to photograph the Tower of London. 'Are you a professional photographer?' the policeman wanted to know. 'Oh no,' said Adams, 'I'm just an *amateur*.' Apocryphal, no doubt, but great.

In the same vein, but infinitely more damaging, is our Official Secrets Act. In what other 'democratic' country could Government-commissioned reports on nutrition be suppressed and committees threatened with the sack if they speak out? Where else can pesticide manufacturers conduct trials which affect all of us and our environment, but have the right to keep the results of their trials secret? Here are just a few mind-boggling quotes from the press in the last few months:

'. . . the committee's report on sugar dangers is covered by the Official Secrets Act.' (*Guardian*)

'Scientists at water authorities have been threatened with criminal proceedings if they talk about costs of dealing with nitrate pollution.' (*Guardian*, during the run-up to water privatisation)

'Britain's big supermarket chains are refusing to inform their customers about pesticides in the food they sell. They carry out massive testing programmes to establish the extent of the contamination of the food on their shelves, but keep the results confidential.' (*Observer*)

'Secret files on pesticide safety are to be opened to manufacturers to increase competition but denied to the public, under proposals announced by the Ministry of Agriculture.' (*Guardian*)

Dr Lacey, the scientist who resigned from a Whitehall committee in December 1989 (see p. 13) is quoted in the *Observer* as saying that he was not allowed to discuss the possible dangers of BST: 'I am bound to secrecy in perpetuity.'

Reports on the economics of both wind and wave power were commissioned and then manipulated or suppressed by the CEGB.

The Government has not divulged the results of any tests before releasing new genetically engineered yeasts into our food and environment; it has not released the results of any tests on food irradiation. Sprays used by the Forestry Commission come under the Official Secrets Act. And so on and on.

Legislation currently going through with the Government's Environmental Protection Bill could go a little way to redress the situation: local registers will publish details of firms which pollute water and air – but there is a catch since firms are worried that commercial information will be made public. David Trippier, Minister for the Environment said: 'We are likely to take a tough line over the definition of commercial information to ensure it is not used to prevent proper monitoring.' This sounds encouraging, if it goes through without too many adjustments. I cannot separate my love of walking and the landscape from my concern over what we are doing to the countryside. We cannot learn to care effectively for the environment until facts are made freely available. In *Index of Censorship* (June/July 1989), Lloyd Timberlake wrote:

'It is impossible to maintain environmental quality and to use environmental resources sustainably without freedom of information. This has been true in the past, is true now, and is the basis for any hope that humankind will be able successfully to cope in the future with new environmental challenges.'

The BBC series *Only One Earth* recommends that governments recognise:
'The right of individuals to know and have access to current information on the state of the environment and natural resources, the right to be consulted and to participate in decision-making on activities likely to have a significant effect upon the environment, and the right to legal remedies and redress for those whose health or environment has been or may be seriously affected.'

In Britain we do not have those rights. It is of the utmost importance that we gain a Freedom of Information Act. Mrs Thatcher has repeatedly stated that we must protect the environment, but we cannot trust the information the Government sees fit to give us – there have been too many economies with the truth. As a nation we require access to facts, figures and issues, so that open and fair debate can ensue, otherwise we are just shadow-boxing, and we will continue our inexorable slide into the shadows of environmental degradation.

In the past, we have been encouraged to die for rural Britain. Recently a friend drew my attention to a remarkable series of First World War posters in the Imperial War Museum. The legend was: 'Your Britain – Fight for it Now.' The pictures were rather sentimental depictions of, for instance, a shepherd with his sheep, large farmhouse in the distance; a pretty English village green; a village fair; thatched cottages and hedged fields. The posters implied that this rural Britain belonged to us, and summoned us to fight and die for it, but it has not been ours for years and, in some cases, centuries. Most of us, however, do carry an image of rural Britain in our hearts, and it's interesting that the Government posters played

on these traditional rural scenes rather than on our great manufacturing cities, our wealthy power base, as they then were.

On the access front we must call for all public rights of way in national parks and National Trust lands to be unblocked immediately, and the rest of the network to be opened by 1995.

On this last matter there have been encouraging developments after recent changes at the Department of the Environment: David Trippier said recently: 'I am very anxious to get across to local authorities the comparison made [in *Managing rights of way: An agenda for action*, published by the Countryside Commission] between the £14 million a year spent on rights of way and the £1 billion spent on tourism, leisure and recreation. We have an important job to do in increasing awareness among local authorities of the importance of rights of way, and of how a great deal can be achieved for a relatively small amount of money.' The Minister gave his support to the target of a 'legally defined, properly maintained and well publicised' rights of way network by the end of the century. David Trippier is possibly one of the few Conservative ministers arguing for an *increase* in expenditure! At last, Government support and encouragement to get out and enjoy the countryside for its own sake. But in comparison with the progress of massive road-building programmes, the end of the century is far too long to wait.

We need to fight for our rights in our forbidden land now. We need to be vigilant, not to take Government information on trust. As a life-long walker I would press for a simple parliamentary bill giving public right of access on foot to open country. We at the Ramblers' Association suggest adapting James Bryce's Access to Mountains (Scotland) Bill of 1884 to read:

'No owner or occupier of open country shall be entitled to exclude any person from walking or being on such land for the purposes of recreation or scientific or artistic study, or to molest him or her in so walking . . .'

Fay Godwin
London, April 1990

It has been a privilege and an honour to be President of the
Ramblers' Association, but I would like to point out that the views
in this book are my own and may not reflect those of the RA.

For further information about the Ramblers' Association
please contact its office at:
1–5 Wandsworth Road, London sw8 2xx. Telephone 071-582 6878.

for the Ramblers' Association
with affection and respect

OUR FORBIDDEN LAND

The Lane

Years and years and man's thoughtful foot,
Drip and guttering rains and mute
Shrinkage of snows, and shaggy-hoofed
Horse have sunk this lane tree-roofed
    Now patched with blossoming elder,
    Wayfaring-tree and guelder;
Lane that eases the sharp-scarped hill
Winding the slope with leisurely will.

Foot of Briton, formal Roman,
Saxon and Dane and Sussex yeoman
Have delved it deep as river-bed,
Till I walk wading to my head
    In air so close and hot
    And by the wind forgot,
It seems to me that in this place
The earth is breathing on my face.

Here I loiter a lost hour,
Listen to bird, look on a flower.
What will be left when I am gone?
A trodden root, a loosened stone
    And by the blackthorn caught
    Some gossamery thought
Of thankfulness to those dead bones
That knit hills closer than loose stones.

Andrew Young

Local footpath, Winchelsea, East Sussex

Most of what little I have learned about British history I've learned through the soles of my feet. Local footpaths are our heritage every bit as much as our historic monuments, as much as Stonehenge: they are pathways through history. They are statutory highways just as much as tarmac roads.

Many landowners, however, are so hostile to the paths that walkers in England and Wales have on average only a *one in three*

chance of being able to complete a 2-mile country walk on rights of way. Approximately *91* per cent of paths which cross cultivated fields in England and Wales are subject to ploughing and planting without being restored as the law requires.

This local crossfield path goes through what was once part of the larger medieval town of Winchelsea, one of the Cinque Ports.

The path goes through the woods and past a ruined priory, and has been connected with other rights of way by Kent Ramblers' Association to form the Saxon Shore Way, a long-distance footpath from Gravesend, round the Kent coast to Rye.

Priory Woods, Kent

Powdermill Woods, near Battle, Kent

Forester Richard Cope set up a woodland
walk through his woods with financial help
from the Countryside Commission. This is
a 'permissive' path, which means that it is
not statutory, and can be closed if the owner
feels there is a fire risk, or it has become too
muddy, if it no longer suits him, or if the
land is sold. Information leaflets are available, and the path also runs through 5 acres
of nature reserve leased to the Sussex Wildlife
Trust.

Winter Woods

air hangs like metal
two swans shrunken
on yellow water
red berries – omens
we cannot decipher
a green leaf startles
                    like blood
whose bones beneath the tree?

we walk – cracking the silence
the daylight moon stares through branches
leprosy invading iron

our warm blood stills
the sun is livid in exile
we have encroached –
this is not yet our land

Frances Horovitz

When I was working on a series of
photographs of the Forest of Dean a few
years ago, there was pressure from the
Ramblers' Association to designate more of
the paths through the forest as statutory
footpaths. The Forestry Commission argued
that since there was unlimited access
throughout the forest (which they own),
there was no need, and I did wonder at the
time why there was so much pressure.

However, the Commission could be
forced to sell off the forest, as they have had
to sell off other lands, or be privatised itself
like the water authorities, so that having
statutory footpaths would safeguard access in
any eventuality. The public could, in theory,
be deprived of access to most of this
magnificent and historic forest as has
happened at Pen Wood on the
Somerset–Dorset border (see p. 17).

Somerset–Dorset border (see p. 17).

Russell's Enclosure, Forest of Dean

Minsmere, Suffolk

At Day-close in November

The ten hours' light is abating,
    And a late bird wings across,
Where the pines, like waltzers waiting,
    Give their black heads a toss.

Beech leaves, that yellow the noon-time,
    Float past like specks in the eye;
I set every tree in my June time,
    And now they obscure the sky.

And the children who ramble through here
    Conceive that there never has been
A time when no tall trees grew here,
    That none will in time be seen.

Thomas Hardy

Walking along the Suffolk Heritage Coast, I was conscious of the squat blocks of Sizewell nuclear power stations and the noisy construction work for Sizewell B which will cost up to £1 million *a day* in higher tax and electricity bills over its estimated thirty-year life. I dropped down into peaceful Minsmere which is an SSSI, an AONB, a Ramsar site, and a proposed special protection area.

There were 4,000 objections to Sizewell B. Over 50,000 had registered opposition to the now-abandoned Sizewell C.

Until recently, a Manpower Services Commission (MSC) warden for these public woods was employed by Bradford City Council. When the Government closed down the MSC the council unfortunately decided not to take over the modest funding and the warden was made redundant. As a result, these valuable edge-of-city woods are now rapidly going downhill. When I went back in the summer, I found fences broken, motor-bike scramblers and Rottweilers all over the place. On my own, I was too nervous to walk there.

Ernest Hall, who rescued nearby Dean Clough at Halifax from dereliction, comments, 'What sometimes depresses me about local government is the contrast between its massive investment in promoting its image and, in this case, its inability to spend a very modest amount of money to conserve these historic woods.'

Wyke Woods, on the edge of Bradford

The Yorkshire Moors

The pearls of a day hung in the topmost height
When my crested hope whistled over drybuilt walls
And I over the good peat and the moss-green bog
Wandered my never-lost way between the calls

Of curlew and playing plover; that was of all
The emptiest world that ever I striding saw,
With a blank road running in the tireless hills
And a day's money to spend, day without flaw.

The heather was young yet and the bilberry leaves
Grew green in the burnt places, bracken was curled
In that flowerless paradise – the stones were the flowers
And the sepal and petal of brilliant water whirled

Under the crag; and over by Ilkley way
I counted, line upon line, rack over rack
The nameless moors I would never walk, and a certain
Concourse of light and cloud which would never come back.

Hal Summers

The network of footpaths in the Bradford–Halifax area is one of the finest in the country, through moors and industrial archaeology, and fewer paths are blocked here than in most other areas. But recently, on the wonderful Calderdale Way, a woman was savaged by two Rottweilers on the first day of her walking holiday. The dogs had already been reported to the police as being dangerous.

Some of these south Pennine moors are now threatened by conifers.

Walls near Queensbury, Bradford

Railway allotments at Saltaire, Bradford

I love footpaths which run past allotments – it's like going through a patchwork of folk art. Allotments became important from the mid-nineteenth century on, after the parliamentary enclosures. As people moved into the cities it soon became apparent that their health was suffering because they were deprived of land to grow food. Local authorities, railway companies and various other bodies and individuals provided the allotments for rent, but often on patronising conditions. For instance, 'Every Occupier will be expected to attend some Place of public Worship at least once on every Sunday, and should he neglect to do so without sufficient cause, will be deprived of his Land.' (From a private contract described in *The Allotment* by David Crouch and Colin Ward.)

Unfortunately the allotments were usually in urban areas where property values were high, so they were often gobbled up by developers. This is now happening faster than ever.

Small farm, Zennor, Cornwall

I used to love walking through a landscape to which I could relate, where animals were not condemned to life imprisonment in cages. Accused of being a romantic, I asked Alan Gear, Chief Executive of the Doubleday Research Association, whether it would ever be possible to feed the whole nation organically. 'I am totally convinced that organic farming is the *only* sustainable way of feeding the population,' was his reply (see p. 15).

'Slowly the branch lines revived, taking advantage of new technologies. As our train passed through the newly subdivided and intensive smallholdings on the beautiful route from Polstead, we realised what a revolution in thinking had taken place. We came to the restored Hadleigh Station through the nature reserve created out of the old line from Hadleigh that was once called the *Railway Walk*.' A Utopian vision of the year 2051 in Suffolk by Ruth Rendell and Colin Ward. (From *Undermining the Central Line*.)

Smallholding near Lydd, Kent

Ripple tip, Gloucestershire

blot in a beauty spot

Ripple tip near Tewkesbury is not only a blot in a beauty spot, there have also been various obstructions to the right of way which goes through it. I visited the tip twice during the summer of 1989, and apart from the forbidding waist-high sheet of corrugated metal blocking the entrance to the path, there were also at least nine dogs loose, some of them Alsatians, which rushed barking on to the road. There have been problems ever since the tip started in 1974: there has been a serious fire and fears of methane gas, and the villagers have tried repeatedly to get it closed down. On one occasion the owner threatened to put 3,000 pigs on the 17-acre site instead.

At the time of going to press I hear that Ripple tip *has* been closed and that problems with methane gas are confirmed, so that it is too dangerous to use the path at all.

These cider orchards near Littledean, in the Forest of Dean, with their grazing sheep and pigs, are threaded with delightful footpaths in accessible Forestry Commission land.

Smallholding near Littledean, Forest of Dean

Since 1983, speculative developers have been submitting ever more ambitious proposals, starting with a few caravans, and now the latest £1-million scheme which includes two-storey holiday homes and a large two-storey leisure centre – a highly damaging intrusion into this unspoilt stretch between Ilkley and Addingham. Wharfedale is in the Ilkley green-belt area just to the north of the heavily populated urban sprawl around Bradford and Leeds, and is also on the route of the Dalesway long-distance footpath.

The planning sagas left me wondering whether we could fairly claim to live in a democracy. The only hope now of averting this development is that it will prove too costly.

Wharfedale, near Ilkley

Reculver Abbey

At an exhibition of my work I was furiously attacked by two Saxon 'experts' for portraying our wonderful Saxon heritage in such an unflattering way. I protested that perhaps they should be attacking the planners, but they maintained it was my responsibility to show our 'heritage' in the best possible light. It makes me wonder what people expect of landscape photographers – it would seem that we are supposed to join in the 'heritage' game to show that everything in the countryside is lovely. The way things are going, if the caravans weren't there, there would no doubt be a 'Heritage Theme Park' along the Saxon Shore Way.

Near Boston, Lincolnshire

East Anglia in general is not a good area for walkers. High guaranteed cereal prices through CAP encouraged farmers into intensive chemical farming, and for many years they were subsidised to remove hedges. Paths were diverted away from their historic routes on to crazy zig-zag lines, and who wants to walk through a chemical prairie anyway?

Farmers are now being subsidised to put back their hedges and, in limited areas, to stop destroying wildlife and polluting water supplies with their chemical sprays and fertilizers.

In this factory-farmed area of Lincolnshire 91 per cent of crossfield paths through arable fields are ploughed up and have not been restored as the law requires. At present, fines for blocked paths are seldom imposed, and are often derisory, sometimes as little as £15.

'As far back as Richard Jefferies . . . writers have wrestled with the difficulties of celebrating natural and rural scenes that were sustained by the blind toil of others. But now the toil is less, and it is nature itself that is being degraded. Our own countryside has become a complicated and powerfully emotive symbol of our precarious life in the world, where we can glimpse some of the diversity and renewal and sense of fittingness increasingly absent from our own lives. That this great repository of values is itself being remorselessly eroded is what makes our concern about its future so great.' (From the Introduction to *In a Green Shade* by Richard Mabey.)

Cholderton Woods after the summer solstice, 1988

When I went to see how Cholderton Woods were left after the 1988 solstice I found English Heritage's 'theme park' approach to Stonehenge almost as offensive as what the revellers left. Now things are set to change with a proposed huge, even more commercialised visitor centre and expensive car park at Larkhill. Visitors will then approach on foot (or possibly in electric cars). Lord Montagu, Chairman of English Heritage, wrote in a letter published in the *Observer*: 'We shall actually enhance the remoteness and mystery of the place. If all goes as we wish, the visitor will see almost nothing of the twentieth century as he [sic] walks towards the stones along the direction of the ancient ceremonial route.'

Amy Hall, Conservative leader of Salisbury Council, has formed an action group in an attempt to block the plan and to preserve the ancient highways of Wessex. The group is called Save Stonehenge (see p. 23).

English Heritage's 'theme park' approach to Stonehenge

Stonehenge, summer solstice 1988

'From the earliest times it has aroused the awe of visitors as one of the wonders of Britain. The monument we see today is the much-ruined final phase of Stonehenge, the prehistoric temple in use some 3,500 years ago.' (From English Heritage's official guide, *Stonehenge and Neighbouring Monuments* by R. J. C. Atkinson.)

Greenham Common

Greenham Common is, as its name implies, common land. The Greenham Women's Peace Camps were set up to protest at the cruise missiles which arrived in 1981, but they also challenged the legality of fencing off the common, and in particular making trespass on common land a criminal offence.

Richard Adams, author of *Watership Down*, wrote in a letter to *The Times* in 1989:

'Now, Greenham Common has ceased to be a nuclear air base and the missiles are all going, so we are told. But the Ministry of Defence intend to retain the air base for reasons that they have never really divulged. The case is fully as unjustifiable as that of Crichel Down in the 1950s.' (For complete letter see p. 21.)

Molesworth

The peace camp established at the Molesworth base, Cambridgeshire, which was preparing to receive cruise missiles, was demolished on 5–6 February 1985 in a midnight military operation involving thousands of soldiers and policemen. There were over 400 vehicles. A CND-proof fence was then erected. The missiles arrived in 1985 and were removed by glasnost in 1988.

'The prospect of nuclear war would, *if we allowed it to*, be totally distracting and depressing. It would *if we allowed it to*, take away the meaning from the rest of our life and finish us off as creative and productive people. It is a prospect which flatly contradicts every other prospect we hold dear . . .' (From *Four Minutes to Midnight* by Nicholas Humphrey.)

The Vandals

The wind is so hot and it blows with such fury
The great pounding waves of the sea sound like thunder –
Not the sea, not the wind but the roar of the silence,
The surge of the blood in your ears.

The night is so dark and the darkness so empty,
No shadow, no shape, no sense of horizon –
Not the night, not the dark, but the harsh stony ridges,
The desert where everything dies.

Is nobody left? Tell me, where has the world gone?
The people, the forests, the great teeming cities –
No people, no houses, no trees and no rivers,
Only this cinder, this slag.

Then what of our hopes, all our dreams, all our strivings,
The dawn of new days with their promise of plenty?
No dreams and no strivings, no past and no future,
All gone, they have wiped the slate clean.

Oh father, dear father, you said that you loved me,
Why did you give them our world for a plaything?
They came with clean hands and they talked so politely
While arranging the death of the world.

They smiled and conspired and we smiled and we let them
Cocooned in the shadows of other men's dreaming;
We gazed at the flickering screens in the half-light
And allowed them to murder the world.

Ewan MacColl

'How can we at one and the same time
declare ourselves for human rights, devote
ourselves to our children, labour to produce
lasting works of art and scholarship *and* take
seriously a vision of the future in which there
are no children, in which our books will
never be read, and our paintings, our houses,
our flower-gardens will end as dust? One or
the other vision has to go.' (From *Four
Minutes to Midnight* by Nicholas Humphrey.)

Faslane Peace Camp

Faslane, home of Trident on Firth of Clyde

In 1985 the Faslane public relations machine put out a long statement through the *Helensburgh Advertiser* which implied that in the unlikely event of an explosion any radioactivity would not penetrate beyond the fence. 'Do they think we are *daft*?' said Ivy Sutherland, secretary of the local amenities society. 'It's so distressing for us, if I mention Coulport to people south of the border, *they have no idea*. I live in the village of Cove at the centre of a triangle of nuclear bases: Faslane, Coulport and Holy Loch. We used to get a lot of pleasure from walking over the hills to neighbouring farms – now all that land is closed off, hundreds of acres, and we resent it' (see p. 20).

Refuse Cruise

Refuse Cruise
and Trident
they're so
unattractive
it's always
more fun
on a
beach
in the
sun
when the
breeze
is not
radio-active

Phil Vallack

Hinkley Point, Somerset

'Chernobyl has forced the Soviet Union to question half a century of Communist belief that technical achievement and productivity are more important than the environment.' (BBC, *Panorama*, 1989.)

I was walking along the seashore near the ancient cinque port of Winchelsea on 3 May 1986, not a million miles from Dungeness or the terrifying rows of French nuclear power stations across the Channel. Although it was a sunny afternoon, there was something strange about the light – a sort of luminous mist, and yet it didn't feel like mist. I regretted not having my camera with me, as I would have liked to explore the light. On the way back to London I heard the news that the radioactive cloud from Chernobyl had passed over the south-east coast. I had walked through it (see p. 21).

Dungeness nuclear power stations, Kent

Morfa Harlech Nature Reserve

Morfa Harlech is one of the finest nature reserves in Wales with many rare birds and waders. Just up river from where the photograph opposite was taken, the power lines from Trawsfynydd nuclear power station cross the estuary.

The power lines over the row of houses at Minffordd may have had a bad effect on local people's health. 'One man committed suicide six years ago, and two other people in this tiny row of houses are being treated for depression,' says writer and photographer Jim Perrin, who lived in the same village.

Dr Cyril Smith, senior lecturer at Salford University's electrical engineering department and author of *Electromagnetic Man*, comments: 'It is now generally accepted that electromagnetic fields, like many other factors, are a biological and medical stressor. In California, estate agents' descriptions of such properties might carry a health risk warning like a packet of cigarettes. However, this risk may escalate into a hazard if, for example, it combines with geopathic stress in the sleeping place. In the north of England a farmer cannot successfully hatch chicks and ducklings on a farm near pylons, he has to incubate and hatch on another farm where there are no power lines over his farm buildings.'

Perhaps in future power lines could be routed over MoD and forestry lands . . .

Trawsfynydd power lines, Minffordd, Penrhyndeudraeth

Beaulieu Estate

The Beaulieu Estate in the New Forest covers 8,000 acres, and Lord Montagu is proud to point out that in 1972 Beaulieu was the first private estate to be made wholly available for educational visits to learn about the environment. About 7,000 children visited during 1989. There is a special bird hide, and the Home Farm has been converted into a residential centre for children from London. According to one head teacher I spoke to, it's a thoroughly good experience for the children.

There is, however, far too little access if you are not a school-child on an educational visit.

The Motor Museum attracts 500,000 visitors a year

There are only 3.5 miles of public footpaths on the 8,000-acre estate in the parish of Beaulieu. Walkers following the Solent Way long-distance footpath hereabouts have to go round by busy twisting narrow roads heavily used by holiday traffic in the summer.

The New Forest is one of the largest and most popular open spaces in the south of England. In 1969 there were 3½ million visitors to its 100 square miles, in 1989 there were at least 8 million. There are plenty of rights of way, but otherwise there is no firmly protected right of access on foot, should the Forestry Commission be forced to privatise the land, or itself be privatised. Commoners who traditionally grazed their ponies, cattle and pigs on the land (which keeps down the scrub and thus protects the character of the forest) now find it uneconomical to do so, and are likely to need subsidies in order to protect the character of the forest. There is considerable pressure from environmental bodies for the New Forest to be given National Park status.

The New Forest

Otmoor, Oxfordshire

Five hundred acres of Otmoor's 4 square miles are taken up by an MoD range. The MoD is proud of the wildlife which flourishes there, and in the summer 1989 issue of *Sanctuary*, their lavishly produced conservation magazine, there are six pages of lyrical descriptions and photographs: 'Otmoor has changed little over the centuries. It still retains its primitive, desolate quiet charm, containing some of the last remnants of habitats once widespread on the moor, and which is secured by the continuing presence of the range.'

Unfortunately much of Otmoor outside the range has been ruined by modern agricultural practice, and many of the footpaths round the moor are blocked.

Wychwood, in Oxfordshire, is called 'the secret forest' because of the lack of public access. In response to pressure from the RA, Oxfordshire County Council finally made a compulsory path creation order for a public right of way just over a mile long, needed to make a good link for a longer round walk. There was a tough public enquiry with much talk about the loss of income to the owner, Lord Rotherwick; but the compensation bill from his Lordship's estate was rather larger than expected – £1.6 million. County councillors had expected a bill for about £25,000. If this preposterous demand were met, it would make it almost impossible for the RA to press for new footpath creation orders elsewhere. In Oxfordshire there are 27,000 acres of woodland, but public access to only 111 acres, a mere 0.4 per cent.

Near Ringstead, north Norfolk

There are not many walkable paths in Norfolk. As far as I know, Lord Peter Melchett is the only landowner to have created new public rights of way on his land, which is now owned by a trust. These have been designated as statutory paths and are marked as such on the Ordnance Survey maps. They are quite different from the 'permissive' paths, 'granted' by the Forestry Commission, the MoD and some private landowners, often in conjunction with visitor centres, small museums and nature trails, which can be closed at any time by the owner.

At Courtyard Farm there are well designed welcoming signs at the gates, and maps and leaflets. I asked Lord Melchett whether the public access had caused any problems on the farm: 'None at all.' What about litter? 'No litter.' Gates left open? (the perpetual moan from farmers about public footpaths). 'The stiles have been very carefully designed and placed, and we find people use them so there is no problem with the gates. There are so few paths in the area we have found that people are coming quite long distances to use them. Perhaps it might be more of a problem if we were closer to heavily populated areas.'

There are two clearly signposted walks, which can be combined to make a third. I was touched to hear that regular walkers had planted bulbs along the paths.

Courtyard Farm, Ringstead

National Nature Reserve on the Cadland Estate

It is a criminal offence to walk along the foreshore on this part of the Heritage Coast, as the NCC has created a National Nature Reserve here, as well as one on part of the foreshore of the Beaulieu Estate. I cannot help wondering whether the NCC might be restricting public access unnecessarily: *A People's Charter?* published by the Countryside Commission suggests: '. . . quiet access on foot is rarely in conflict with conservation, apart from a small number of particularly popular places where erosion can occur.' What's more, by designating the nature reserves where it has, the NCC has precluded the possibility of a continuous foreshore path, so that walkers on the Solent Way have to walk some distance round on tarmac roads.

The Courtyard Farm Trust has put two public hides on to its grazing marshes. Peter Melchett writes in *Making Tracks* '. . . some of the best nature reserves have footpaths going through or round them, and organisations like the RSPB are building public hides on their reserves, with tracks leading to them from public footpaths. The number of instances where there is any genuine difficulty caused by access is tiny.'

The long-distance coastal footpaths, the Peddars Way and North Norfolk Coast Path, go through land managed by the Norfolk Naturalists' Trust, the National Trust, and the NCC, and no apparent damage to the wildlife has been reported since the paths were opened.

During 1988 Peter Melchett, then
Vice-Chairman of the Ramblers'
Association, publicly accused the army of
unlawfully blocking a number of footpaths at
Lydd in Kent. 'This is theft,' he said. The
footpaths were eventually reopened, but in
such a way that few members of the public
would wish to use them; certainly not a place
to take toddlers for a Sunday afternoon walk.

The army then tried to close the paths
legally with the aid of Kent County Council.
But instead of adopting the open approach of
a public inquiry, the council tried the unusual
procedure of applying to the local
magistrates' court. The council submitted a
flawed and poorly prepared case; in spite of
the RA pointing out why they *could not*
legally close the paths, the magistrates went
ahead and did so.

The RA appealed successfully to the High
Court. Not only did the High Court back the
public, but Lord Justice Woolf stated that 'In
a case of this nature, the Ramblers'
Association are in effect representing the
public and are performing, so to speak, a
public service.'

Footpaths illegally closed by the military at Lydd

Old Winchester Hill, Hampshire

Old Winchester Hill is now a National Nature Reserve, owned by the NCC. The reserve was used as a practice mortar-range from 1940 to 1945. There is now limited public access to parts of the reserve, the rest of which cannot be cleared because military 'resources are limited' (but not when it comes to building Trident or acquiring new land for the MoD). There is a four-sided NCC leaflet with such reassuring headings as, 'What to do if you find a bomb' – this on the area *cleared* for access.

Stanford Training Area (*opposite*) is one of the largest training areas in the country to include live firing. In 1942 the inhabitants of six villages were moved out on the understanding that they would be allowed back after the war, but they never have been. Now the MoD states that Stanford, acre for acre, is one of the most intensively used training areas in the UK and is proud of its conservation on the range; it brings in coach-loads to a visitor centre, but there is too much unexploded ammunition to allow unaccompanied public access.

The God of War

I saw the old god of war stand in a bog between chasm and rockface.

He smelled of free beer and carbolic and showed his testicles to adolescents, for he had been rejuvenated by several professors. In a hoarse wolfish voice he declared his love for everything young. Nearby stood a pregnant woman, trembling.

And without shame he talked on and presented himself as a great one for order. And he described how everywhere he put barns in order, by emptying them.

And as one throws crumbs to sparrows, he fed poor people with crusts of bread which he had taken away from poor people.

His voice was now loud, now soft, but always hoarse.

In a loud voice he spoke of great times to come, and in a soft voice he taught the women how to cook crows and seagulls. Meanwhile his back was unquiet, and he kept looking round, as though afraid of being stabbed.

And every five minutes he assured his public that he would take up very little of their time.

Bertolt Brecht

Pop-up target, Stanford training area, Norfolk

Abereiddy, Pembrokeshire Coast National Park

Abereiddy Bay on the north coast of the Pembrokeshire Coast National Park includes a marvellous stretch of the coastal footpath, but some of the south coast is blighted by the extensive Castlemartin ranges. Many of the most remarkable stacks such as Pen-y-Holt are in the military exclusion area, though a few small concessions to access, such as accompanied group walks in the summer months, have been offered by the military in recent years. Much of the coastal path though is forced on to tarmac roads inland.

There are wrecked tanks littered around on the Castlemartin ranges. When I stopped to photograph Romulus, a 65-ton Conqueror tank which was in service from 1958 to 1963, just outside the Merrion Camp, I was immediately approached by a guard who wanted to know what I was doing, even though the tank is a tourist attraction.

Romulus, Merrion Camp, Pembrokeshire Coast National Park

But come. Grief must have its term? Guilt too, then.
And it seems there is no limit to the resourcefulness of recollection.
So that a man might say and think:
When the world was at its darkest,
When the black wings passed over the rooftops
(And who can divine His purposes?) even then
There was always, always a fire in this hearth.
You see this cupboard? A priest-hole!
And in that lumber-room whole generations have been housed and fed.
Oh, if I were to begin, if I were to begin to tell you
The half, the quarter, a mere spattering of what we went through!

James Fenton
from *A German Requiem*

Tyneham was requisitioned by the MoD during the Second World War with the (unfulfilled) promise that it would be returned to the villagers after the war. Following local protest and national media coverage, the MoD has finally created a walk through the village, open on certain days; it has also patched up the houses damaged by ricocheting shells, and made a small museum. A new way of joining the heritage industry?

Meticulously restored house at Tyneham

Willsworthy Camp, Dartmoor

Dartmoor has been one of the most embattled of the national parks; recently it was badly damaged by a slice being taken out of it by the Okehampton Bypass by a cynical Department of Transport. Now there are further battles between the MoD and environmentalists, headed by the veteran campaigner Lady Sayer, whose family has lived on Dartmoor for more than a century. The MoD wants to build permanent stone-built and slated barracks at Willsworthy on land which they purchased *inside* the national park. It would clearly prejudice the Duchy of Cornwall's deliberations as to whether to renew permission for military use of adjacent land if there were a permanent barracks, as opposed to the Willsworthy 'Camp' which is of a more 'temporary' nature, even though it has been in hideous place for over forty years.

A few years ago the National Trust decided not to renew the licence for military training on its Dartmoor land. Can live firing in a national park ever be justified? It has been argued that the military has been on Dartmoor for far longer than the national park, but there is a distressing list of accidents – four of them fatal between 1953 and 1966 – and near-accidents with live ammunition. SSSIs and prehistoric sites have been damaged in the past. Even the experienced walker, Chris Brasher, found himself in crossfire on Dartmoor after walking up the beautiful Tavy Cleave valley. 'I didn't want to go to hell just yet,' he says, so he got out his mobile phone and was able to alert the military to his presence; but what of the ordinary punter who doesn't carry such technological wonders when out for a walk on the moors?

With the exception of Exmoor, there are military holdings in every single national park. It is bad enough having live firing in a national park, but even worse to think that training exercises with radioactive materials could also be going on. Although they are only carried out on MoD-owned land, it would be reassuring to know that they are not carried out on Willsworthy; but General Jeapes, the GOC South-west District is not 'at liberty' to give this reassurance, which would surely be helpful for public relations on Dartmoor, or other national parks.

On one of the days I spent on Dartmoor several military vehicles raced past me on the track near Willsworthy Camp; at about 5 p.m. coach-loads of soldiers with blackened faces and overnight camping bags were unloaded into the public car park near the Merrivale prehistoric circles and barrows. The men bristled with guns and I found their presence on an August Sunday afternoon both offensive and intimidating. Had I come down off the moor a little later, I would have encountered them up there and been even more nervous, although I knew that firing was not scheduled to start until after midnight.

'The fighting services are bound to become serious enemies of what is left of England. Wherever they see a tract of wild, unspoiled country they naturally want it for camps, artillery practice, bomb-dropping, poison gas tests.' E. M. Forster

Merrivale barrows and stone rows, Dartmoor

In response to persistent hostile criticism that they were damaging our heritage, the army has protected the prehistoric barrows from target practice, sightseers and – photographers . . .

Everleigh Barrows, Wiltshire

Nine Maidens Stones, West Penwith

A few years ago many of the prehistoric monuments around Zennor were defaced with large whitewashed numbers.

When painter Patrick Heron first covenanted his land to the National Trust in about 1959, the Trust enlisted his aid to fight off a military threat from RNAS Culdrose to use the land for training. That campaign was won, although Heron describes the crude tactics used by the military to harass him, such as sending groups of from four to eight helicopters at a time to hang motionless but noisily over his house, barely 50 feet up; and also over fellow artist Bryan Wynter's home, for long periods, after which they requested that Wynter should stop throwing stones at the helicopters. (Wynter retorted that the helicopters shouldn't be close enough to throw stones *at*.)

Problems with RNAS Culdrose surfaced again in 1982 when the Trust was feeling particularly patriotic – soon after the misguided Bradenham Bunker affair when inalienable land was leased to the MoD – and just post-Falklands. Heron describes groups of uniformed trainees tramping over his covenanted NT land, and at the same time large whitewashed numbers appeared on the prehistoric monuments around Zennor

continued

though the military denied any involvement in these. Heron got in touch with the Trust, again expecting support in fighting off the military, only to be told by its area agent about RNAS Culdrose's 'present need' which 'comes at a time when it is only because we have, thank God, had highly trained troops which have received precisely this sort of training that we have avoided military and political disaster.' The letter infuriated Heron, a lifelong pacifist.

Heron never got a clear answer to his question, posed to Lord Gibson, Chairman of the NT at that time: 'What all of us in Zennor who have granted the National Trust restrictive covenants over our land feel we now have a right to know is whether the National Trust, as a matter of national policy, is prepared to grant free use and access to the armed forces to all covenanted lands?' Altogether Heron has fought and won no fewer than eleven major campaigns to safeguard his land and other sites nearby. I asked him what protection covenanting land to the National Trust conferred. 'So far as I can see, now, none at all, it merely stops the *owner* changing the character of the land.'

But even that is not always the case: this summer I saw a farmer using a bulldozer to remove huge submerged boulders from his tiny Bronze-Age fields on land covenanted to the Trust. The farmer is also in receipt of Environmentally Sensitive Area subsidies. Looking down on the patchwork of tiny fields, when the slanting sun caught them, was to look on a jewelled landscape. This has now all been ripped apart, and huge boulders placed in ugly heaps around the field. Heron alerted the Trust, but no action was taken. I spoke to John Brookes, National Trust Head Warden for West Penwith. 'The Trust is in the unenviable position of trying to interpret the covenants which state that they should not impede agriculture following a traditional form of management. Since rocks have traditionally been removed, it is difficult to stop the practice now, even though there are very few of these tiny Bronze-Age fields left.'

One would like to welcome ESAs, but looking at how they are being implemented by MAFF in West Penwith, I am dubious. Owners adjacent to Heron have common grazing rights. This starts to get complicated when for example an owner who is not a farmer and owns no animals 'rents' a farmer's animals in order to enter into an ESA agreement and claim the subsidy. Just as farmers have sold their milk quotas, so farmers are now selling or buying ESA subsidies. The fear is that Heron's 140 acres of covenanted NT land could be fenced and grazed for the first time in living memory. The land, with paths, would still be available to the public, but this is not an 'environmentally sensitive' way to treat land.

There are also plans to spoil the lovely Zennor road with lay-bys, but there is a perfectly adequate car park at Zennor. What is more, footpath signs on 5-foot high wooden posts are being erected across the small moors, ruining the skylines, even though the ESA policy statement says that the walks will be signposted on stiles and with low granite boulders.

There are many excellent leaflets about the archaeology of the area, but now: 'Preliminary discussions with English Heritage and the County Archaeologist indicate interpretative information will be provided and maintained, in a discreet noticeboard format in each site area.' (MAFF/ESA Interim Statement.) No doubt West Penwith will be turned into a giant theme park. Can nothing at all be left to the imagination, for us to discover individually, leaflet in hand, for us to photograph without the intrusion of 'discreet noticeboard' labels?

It is ironic that a pacifist should have had to fight so many campaigns and lawsuits to safeguard his beloved landscape during the last thirty years. Although we must be thankful that Heron has succeeded so far, I cannot help being saddened at the loss of time and energy from his life as a painter. And of course I'm concerned that he now feels that there is no way a landowner can safeguard land for posterity.

Zennor Quoit on Patrick Heron's National Trust land

Augury

The fish faced into the current,
Its mouth agape,
Its whole head opened like a valve.
You said 'It's diseased.'

A pale crusted sore
Turned like a coin
And wound to the bottom,
Unsettling silt off a weed.

We hang charmed
On the trembling catwalk:
What can fend us now
Can soothe the hurt eye

Of the sun,
Unpoison great lakes,
Turn back
The rat on the road.

Seamus Heaney

Warehouse demolition in run-down Hayle, west Cornwall

'Cornwall has so much potential it's unbelievable. When you think how people are falling over themselves in the south-east for a tiny parcel of development, Cornwall is a goldmine,' (Peter de Savary). Apart from the theme park at Land's End, already established, Mr de Savary is planning a massive shopping development at Falmouth, and a huge housing scheme at Hayle Estuary. 'Will de Savary, who owns the land round the vast estuary, give Hayle the devastating face-lift he has given Land's End, and similarly remove every trace of its ancient character?' (Stephen Gardiner in the *Observer*).

'One cannot help feeling that the sort of employment the majority of the present residents of Hayle will find coming their way if de Savary's dream of a sort of Cornish "Port Grimaud" ever comes about will be window-cleaning, refuse-collecting, car-park tending. They will rapidly feel like second-class citizens . . .' (Patrick Heron).

'Twenty-six years ago Geoffrey Moorhouse in *The Other England* reproduced a letter which had been published in the *West Briton and Royal Cornwall Gazette*:

'Sometimes the "foreigners" even come to stay – or retire – and because of them we find we can no longer afford the high prices asked for houses in the seaside villages where we were born and brought up. Would that next summer not half but all of Cornwall's visitors stayed away. There would be hardship, but we could recover from it and would then be forced to base our future on more wholesome foundations, no longer titillated into dallying with this painted lady of the holiday trade. We could bequeath to our children, too, a way of life in which they could find more pride and satisfaction.'

Peter de Savary's Land's End

'. . . of all the places where the visitor feels the real spirit of Cornwall, Land's End stands unique. Nowhere else is the majesty of the sea more apparent. Nowhere else gives quite the same sensation of oneness with nature. Nowhere else has quite the same strange mixture of mystery, legend, drama and sheer beauty.' (From *A Pictorial Souvenir of Land's End*, published by the Management of the Land's End estate.)

Land's End car park – off to John o'Groats?

Ramblers' Association Chairman Chris Hall addresses a rally at Milldale

At a Forbidden Britain rally at Milldale in the Peak District Chris Hall, Chairman of the Ramblers' Association, said:

'The National Trust rejoices in its huge membership ("I'm one in a million" proclaim the car-stickers). It lovingly watches the league table of admissions to its stately homes.

'But if you want access to land where the Trust does not at present admit you, there may be problems.

'Walkers can follow the banks of the delectable Dove, down Beresford Dale, Wolfscote Dale, Milldale and Dovedale itself. The route is a justly famous jewel in the crown of British scenic beauty. But anyone following this walk must for half a mile – between Lode Mill and Viators Bridge – walk on the road. This can be dangerous, smelly, unpleasant.

'The Trust owns the opposite bank where people *could* walk, but refuses to open a path there. The Trust claims the path would interfere with its tenant-farmer's sheep. But sheep and walkers coexist over half northern England. It would get in the way, says the Trust, of fly-fishing – but the Trust must decide whether it gives priority to walkers or a handful of sportsmen on its property.

'But here is the nub. The Trust claims to have a policy of keeping one side of the river "undamaged, uncluttered". It fears the path would be used by "day-trippers" visiting Milldale.

'If people are clutter and "day-trippers" are a problem, then the Trust is in the wrong business.'

National Trust's Milldale in the Peak District

Forest of Bowland

walking is Britain's most popular outdoor recreation

'If they [the Ramblers' Association] want a green field to walk on, or solitude from now on, they must work hard, save up and buy it. Until ramblers come to terms with the fact that they are not universally liked, we must be prepared for more tragedies of the sort we have just seen in Pembrokeshire.' (Auberon Waugh in the *Spectator*, July 1989, after two ramblers were shot dead on the Pembrokeshire Coast Path.)

In the 62 square miles of the Forest of Bowland, Lancashire County Council has achieved only limited access. Much of the forest is owned by the Duke of Westminster, said to be the richest man in the UK. There are footpaths mainly on the lower ground round Abbeystead House, but very limited access to the moors which are used for shooting. 'After every Bank Holiday I have to clear up the Trough – after the last Bank Holiday weekend we took out 2½ tons of litter,' said the Duke in a TV *Skyline* interview with Muriel Gray.

'It is completely unreasonable in the last decade of the twentieth century for a small number of landowners to expect to be able to bar the public from their land. Access must be accompanied by an expectation of good behaviour, and of an attitude of respect for the land and the life it supports. But that attitude will not arise unless the access is provided. Until it is, there will always be a resentment that we are denied, for no good reason, that which we could enjoy, appreciate and respect.' (From *A People's Charter?* published by the Countryside Commission.)

The Duke of Westminster's Estate, Forest of Bowland

Cefn y Griafolen, Wales

I walked up the mid-Wales valley on a glorious January morning, feeling privileged and delighted to be there. Until the screaming jets shattered everything.

Only Britain, of the European NATO allies, allows jets to fly as low as 100 feet in some areas.

'Who has ever been forbidden to wander over an alp? Who has ever been threatened with an interdict in the Apennines? Who has ever been warned off the rocks of the Tyrol? Who has ever been prosecuted for trespassing among Norwegian mountains?' asked Charles Trevelyan MP in 1908 when he introduced a bill to create rights of access to Britain's open country.

An amateur photographer was standing a foot or two off the public footpath at Rainster Rocks which have always been popular with climbers, when the landowner (with dog) came across the field and ordered him to take his film out. Astonished, the walker asked why. The landowner explained that he didn't want any publicity or any more people coming to his rocks. If he had his way, there wouldn't be any ramblers there at all. The landowner rents out his land but keeps a close eye on it. Recently he has erected head-high posts to mark the line of one of the paths; he feels so strongly that ramblers should not deviate from the right of way that he may even fence it in if too many step off the path for whatever reason, or behave badly in some way. Recently, also, two new notices have appeared to the effect that payment of £5 will allow a climb on the rocks.

Brassington, Derbyshire

The quarry is being restored according to plans agreed with the Peak Park Planning Board. The line of the working may be left to form a small limestone dale. Despite the scale of the operations the tree in the middle distance has been preserved. The scheme shows how jobs can be provided, a necessary mineral obtained and the landscape restored to an appearance that will be, if not identical to, at any rate of the same character as that which existed before. The supervision of land restoration after fluorspar working has been one of the Peak Park's particular successes.

Fluorspar quarry, Bradwell

Helwith Bridge Quarry, Horton in Ribblesdale

This is the first quarry in the Yorkshire Dales National Park area to cut through the skyline, completely altering the shape of the hill. The quarry has recently gained extended planning permission and the last relict wood in the area has been destroyed. 'My own feeling on quarrying in the national parks is that it should never be allowed. Once the landscape is destroyed it is destroyed for ever. The parks are there to serve the needs and interests of the nation and not just of the multinationals out to make, as always, the maximum profit regardless of the destruction.' (Mike Harding.)

Footpath 56 at Pye Bridge used to be delightful, flanked by tall Lombardy poplars, but hauliers have moved on to the adjacent site, and the path has become an eyesore. Residents complain that lorries cross the path most weekdays.

A footpath diversion was applied for about three years ago, and the district council footpath officer states that the now ruined path will eventually be diverted, but that it may take some time in view of objections – including some from British Coal – on safety grounds. Meanwhile, local residents may have several more years of misery.

Footpath 56 at Pye Bridge, Belper, Derbyshire

Castle steel works, Bradwell, Peak District

This is the view from a popular walking lane, Outlands Head, above Bradwell in the Peak District National Park. The Peak Park Planning Board imposed landscaping conditions to screen the site, but they have not been properly complied with. The hard-pressed Board is having to use its slender resources to enforce them.

Just across the lane, residents of Bradwell are opposing the dumping of deadly asbestos in the Outlands Head Quarry.

Quarries and Fleetwith Pike on the way to Haystacks, Cumbria

The Lake District was rejected as a candidate for a World Heritage Site because it is under so many pressures such as low-level flying, quarrying and tourism. It is being resubmitted as a 'Cultural Heritage Site' as opposed to a 'natural' – landscape – site. This is due to its 'cultural' associations with Wordsworth, Coleridge, Beatrix Potter and others, all of whom came, of course, to the Lake District because of its natural beauty.

The pressures on this national park area have been enormous, especially recently from developers. Although many development plans were rejected by the Lake District National Park, 47 per cent of those decisions which went to appeal were overturned by the Government during 1987–8, presumably on their *laissez-faire* policy. There are over twenty tourist complexes including time-share developments;

it is now so grossly overcrowded that on the May Bank Holiday in 1989 the Lake District was closed to cars.

Haystacks is one of the favourite walks described by the great artist and guide A. Wainwright; he is said to have declared that he would like his ashes scattered around 'Innominate Tarn' at the top.

Rare limestone pavements like this one at
Twistleton Scar are under threat – recently
about half an acre of similar scar in Lower
Ribblesdale was removed for use as
rock-garden material, even though it was in
the national park.

Karst limestone pavement and Ingleborough

Stubble burning is obnoxious; it is dangerous to walkers and motorists; it is damaging to wildlife, and sometimes destroys hedges and hedgerow trees; and the smoke and smuts cause great nuisance to people living near by.

In December 1989, John Gummer, Minister for Agriculture, announced: 'The Government has therefore decided that straw and stubble burning shall be banned' (with effect from after the 1992 harvest). But the March 1990 issue of *Environmental Health News* reports that in its amendment to the Environmental Protection Bill, the Government states that 'exemptions may be applicable: in all, or in specified areas, to all or only to specified crop residues; or to all or in specified circumstances.'

Stubble will continue to be a burning issue.

Stubble burning, east Kent

Dying trees, Northumberland

The Middleton family bungalow in Loscoe, Derbyshire, was blown up in 1986 by methane gas from the neighbouring landfill site. I have never seen so many 'For Sale' boards up anywhere as in Loscoe. Not only is the landfill site in the centre of the village, there are up to four blasts a day at the huge open-cast coal mine across the road.

I spoke to one of Loscoe's residents who said: 'I have got a monitor on my building which has recorded explosive levels more than once, and if I wanted to sell my property they'd take one look and say "Oh dear!" Although the council are trying to do their best, they've been, they've tested, but I'm quite sure that eventually there will be health problems. I keep complaining about the smells, but they're often at 4 a.m. and how can I get the council here at 4 a.m.? We don't know what's in the tip, it's top secret, everything is top secret – they let you know just what they want you to know. With all the trouble we've had, it's changed the way we behave – I've got much more aggressive and outspoken than I ever was before. How *dare* they bring waste in from abroad when they can't deal with our own waste! [see p. 46].

'All our family have now got big sores up our noses – the council are only testing for methane, but there must be some other poison – the council say there's no proof . . . they should tell us *exactly* what is in the tip – we've got children, all of us, it's not just us, it's our children, and our children's children.' The speaker has asked me to withhold her name because she feared that her comments might affect a possible sale of her property . . .

A council official commented that waste tips must now be located in rural not residential areas, but although fewer people may be in danger, there are still problems, especially with water.

The Middletons' house at Loscoe

'I didn't consider I might be poisoned'

What the Serpent Said to Adam

If the sky is infected
The river has to drink it

If earth has a disease that could be fatal
The river has to drink it

If you have infected the sky and the earth
Caught its disease off you – you are the virus

If the sea drinks the river
And the earth drinks the sea

It is one quenching and one termination

If your blood is trying to clean itself
In the filter of your flesh
And the sores run – that is the rivers

The five rivers of Paradise

Where will you find a pure drink now?

Already, look, the drop has returned to the cup

Already you are your ditch, and there you drink

Ted Hughes

'Our rivers are corridors for life in the countryside,' said Andrew Lees of Friends of the Earth. 'They are where our most important wildlife exists, and they supply 70 per cent of our drinking water.' The River Aire is one of the most polluted in Britain. In 1986 two policemen dived in to save a drowning man, and one was still off work a year later. 'I started to be very ill, with vomiting and very bad diarrhoea and a sort of sleepiness, very tired all the time, headaches . . . I have never ever been as poorly as that. Before I went in I did consider that I might drown, but I didn't consider that I might be poisoned.' (From Radio Four's *Face the Facts*: 'Water', July 1987.)

The Aire is not unique, there is growing evidence to suggest that many of our rivers, our bathing beaches and even our drinking water supplies are becoming so badly polluted as to constitute a threat to public health.

Shipley Fields, Bradford

River Aire from public footpath at Shipley, Bradford

Pont Scethin, a medieval pack-horse bridge in the Snowdonia National Park, is in a designated ancient landscape area. For me this was some of the most beautiful landscape in the whole of the UK, and I used a picture of the bridge on the front cover of my book *The Drovers' Roads of Wales* (with Shirley Toulson). So I was dismayed and saddened when I received a seven-page typed new year's day 1989 letter from Jim Perrin, writer and photographer, telling in elegiac terms of the destruction of the Bronze-Age tracks around Pont Scethin by the Welsh Water Authority in the run-up to privatisation, leaving 'a scar, a dark slash, a quagmire in places fifty yards wide . . . the sparse mountain vegetation will not recover in my lifetime. We live in an age when public utilities such as water (the land for which was taken from people, for the most part by compulsion, for the greater good) must now be modernised and made efficient in order to be sold off for private profit. And when that has happened the land must be made to pay, so the public could be excluded.'

Jim Perrin invited me to walk to Pont Scethin with him, and subsequently published an account of our walk and conversation in *Climber & Hillwalker* magazine. This, and our protests through the RA, resulted in an apology from the Welsh Water Authority and in their making costly efforts to repair the damage; I understand that although the Bronze-Age tracks as they were have gone for ever, at least the scars are now healing. The public has not been excluded yet; we hope it never will be (see p. 18).

Pont Scethin area being prepared for water privatisation

Great Yarmouth is an ancient town on a tongue of land between two rivers, with golden sandy beaches which have traditionally been a popular resort for the midlands. Recently, however, there have been problems with sewage.

About four years ago an unfortunate yachtsman visiting the Norfolk Broads came to Great Yarmouth and accidentally moored under one of the thirty-four or so sewage outlets going into the rivers Bure and Yare. The tide went down and so did his boat, and when he woke up it was filled with raw sewage. A local doctor was concerned at the threat to public health, so he painted a warning by the outfall in large white letters: 'DANGER RAW SEWAGE!' The council was understandably concerned about the effects this would have on tourism, and blacked it out. The doctor persevered with the notices and was eventually caught. The council was going to have him bound over for defacing public property, but thought better of it, realising the publicity this would cause.

At the time the water authority was preparing to pipe it into long-sea outfalls, passing it through a 6-millimetre square mesh, but the strained sewage will still be untreated. Pat Gowen, North Sea Co-ordinator, Norfolk Friends of the Earth: 'It's more dangerous on three grounds, the most important of which is that the casual holiday-maker who looks at the high tideline thinks it's a clean beach – all the tell-tales have been removed – and thus it's more dangerous because holiday-makers are more likely to go in.' In 1959 the Royal Commission on Environmental Pollution put out a statement: 'There should be no threat to public health on the proviso that the bathing water is not so polluted as to be aesthetically revolting.' This proviso, says Gowen, has not been updated in thirty years, even with the advent of screened and therefore invisible sewage.

I asked if the sewage sludge could be used for fertilizer, and heard that in 1983 the Government gave the go-ahead to the chemical industries to combine their industrial waste (containing heavy metals) with the domestic sewage; this makes it poisonous as fertilizer, so that's why they dump it into the sea. Pure domestic sewage makes very good fertilizer, which needs no added nitrates and thus saves polluting water supplies. There are also new plants in America which turn the sludge into usable and even saleable products. The capital costs of many of these plants are low, far less than conventional sewage-treatment plants, quite small in scale, and often less in both installation and running costs than long-sea untreated outfalls. But industry would first have to stop pouring their chemical waste into the domestic sewage system.

Update on going to press: finally Britain has agreed (March 1990) to stop burning waste on the North Sea and that sewage discharge by long-sea outfall should eventually be treated but there is still no date. In March 1990 Pat Gowen presented a paper to a House of Commons Committee to the effect that scientists had found that the HIV Aids virus can survive in sewage-polluted sea water for at least twenty-four hours.

Not only is it dangerous to swim in British waters, inland or coastal, they are so contaminated in places that they are also a hazard to people on the beach and to walkers along the coast. Sea spray can carry bacteria and viruses, some of which can live for up to seventeen months even in the chilly North Sea.

Pat Gowen again: 'Hygienic sewage-disposal is an essential common right of a civilised society.'

River Bure, Great Yarmouth, 1989

'We have made it [the North Sea] into a rubbish dump. The effluents we pour heedlessly into its waters are a threat to its delicate ecological balance . . . while we wait for the doctor's diagnosis, the patient may easily die,' HRH the Prince of Wales at North Sea Pollution Conference in London in 1987.

'Britain is the only country now dumping untreated sewage sludge into the North Sea,' Pat Gowen, North Sea Co-ordinator, Norfolk Friends of the Earth.

'It's treated sewage of course –' Margaret Thatcher, BBC2, *Nature*, 1989.

At the popular and beautiful beach at Bude in north Cornwall, B & B owners warn visitors to keep out of the water because raw sewage is pumped across the beach. In Britain most local councils are reluctant to publicise dirty beaches because of the damage to the tourist industry, but in this case local councillor Brenda Parsons was featured on a TV AM programme wearing a yellow shirt with the legend 'Costa del Excreta'. Now a new 1,000-metre outfall is being built at Bude which will marginally reduce pollution, but may be more dangerous because the strained but still untreated sewage will be invisible, and so people will be less careful.

In Denmark there is a special department to deal with bathing waters: polluted beaches are advertised everywhere, including libraries and schools.

Bude, Cornwall

The sea has encroached over the 5,000-year-old forests on this beach, but at low tide the tree roots, covered in marine life, still show. Now pollution is also encroaching on this beach which has been awarded a 'pass' by the Tidy Britain Group.

Pett Level, East Sussex

Looking north from Summerhouse Hill, near tunnel works

ruining the Garden of England

Mrs Thatcher and President Mitterrand signed the Channel Tunnel agreement in Canterbury Cathedral; the Government's terms precluded any public inquiry, and no provision for environmental consultation was stipulated. The works have been decided by commercial considerations more than by regional planning.

The tunnel works impinge on three SSSIs, and many plants and wildlife habitats are under threat. Eurotunnel have expediently put out a handsome brochure: *The Channel Tunnel and your Environment*, outlining some of the concessions they have voluntarily made, and measures they have taken to 'mitigate the effects of construction as far as is practicable'. The works for the tunnel on their own probably could be absorbed by the countryside. But by siting the terminal so far south, the relentless pressure of new roads, rail links, warehousing and other infrastructure will ruin the Garden of England.

Summerhouse Hill and Channel Tunnel works

Thirty years ago porpoises used to come into the shallows here. Now they've gone, although dolphins can still occasionally be seen. Nobody knows why this small whale died a couple of years ago, perhaps it was stranded, perhaps it was the state of the sea.

Fishermen along the south coast, especially around Hastings and Hythe, are suffering from incapacitating eye and skin diseases which they say they first got after being drenched in sea spray and handling fishing-nets near sewage outfalls along the Channel coast.

Stranded whale, Winchelsea Beach, East Sussex

The Government has appropriated draconian powers with the Channel Tunnel Bill, and it is pushing through a new dual carriageway along the cliffs between Capel le Ferne and Dover on the Bill; its own Department of Transport had pointed out earlier that it would be extremely expensive. It will also be environmentally damaging, and is likely to save only about one-and-a-half minutes. In fact the case for this road was *reduced* by the Channel Tunnel as the terminal is sited well before the cliffs, so the Government should never have pushed it through on the Channel Tunnel Bill. Mark Sullivan, CPRE adviser on transport says: 'This is an abuse of power.'

The North Downs Way runs along the cliffs which will be ruined by the new dual carriageway. This is one of the finest coastal landscapes in England, designated as Heritage Coast by the Countryside Commission, and part of the Kent Downs AONB, meriting special protection.

The spoil is being dumped at the bottom of Shakespeare Cliff; there is more coming out per mile than expected so Eurotunnel want an extension to the terraces.

There are many concerns about safety: On *The London Programme*, Peter Gribbin, Chief Fire Officer from Surrey said: 'I am a professional fire officer with twenty-nine years' experience. I have a deep feeling that desegregation [of cars and passengers] is inherently dangerous and I would not wish to travel in such a manner, nor would I wish my family to travel in such a manner. I simply urge the authorities to consider safety and not set it aside when it begins to concern itself perhaps with profit and loss.'

And on the same programme, Dave Matthews, National Health and Safety Officer, Fire Brigades Union, said: 'The Union forecast such incidents and disasters as the Bradford football fire, Hillsborough, King's Cross Underground fire, and on the Channel Tunnel we predict that if legislation is not put into place before it's up and running, then legislation will only be forthcoming after another disaster and subsequent loss of life.'

Dover Cliffs, North Downs Way and tunnel works

All The World's Beauty

all the world's
beauty

salmon-leaping
up and over all
the huge chill wall
of the waterfall
where hurtling water
sprays and foams on the deep
and deepening dip
in the limestone's mouth
and on the limestone's lip

all the world's
beauty

yes i saw it all
like a washed ghost
out of the corner
of my timid eye

all the world's
beauty

but no i couldn't turn
myself around to bask in it –
i knew my duty:
to watch black tarmac miles of motorway
for the columns of the killers
willing themselves along to kill

all the world's
beauty

Adrian Mitchell

Meall Mòr, Glencoe

The Government plans to spend £12 billion on building new roads throughout Britain and widening existing motorways and trunk roads by the end of the century; so what will be left? There is also tremendous pressure for more ski developments in the Cairngorms. These will generate more pressure for roads and residential developments and will threaten fragile Arctic environments.

After presenting the Better Environment Awards for Industry to ICI, Sainsbury's and other companies, Mrs Thatcher said: 'We are not going to do away with the great car economy . . .' (see p. 22).

Landscape and I

Landscape and I get on together well.
Though I'm the talkative one, still he can tell
His symptoms of being to me, the way a shell
Murmurs of oceans.

Loch Rannoch lapses dimpling in the sun.
Its hieroglyphs of light fade one by one
But re-create themselves, their message done,
For ever and ever.

That sprinkling lark jerked upward in the blue
Will daze to nowhere but leave himself in true
Translation – hear his song cascading through
His disappearance.

The hawk knows all about it, shaking there
An empty glove on steep chutes of the air
Till his yellow foot cramps on a squeal, to tear
Smooth fur, smooth feather.

This means, of course, Schiehallion in my mind
Is more than mountain. In it he leaves behind
A meaning, an idea, like a hind
Couched in a corrie.

So then I'll woo the mountain till I know
The meaning of the meaning, no less. Oh,
There's a Schiehallion anywhere you go.
The thing is, climb it.

Norman MacCaig

Stob Dubh, Glen Etive, Glencoe

Es war einmal

I raised my gun
I took the sight
Against the sun
I shot a kite.

I raised my gun
I took the sight
A second one
I shot in flight.

I raised my gun
I shot a plover
I loaded up
And shot another.

Now round about me
Lay the dead
One more, one more,
Then home to bed.

Pray Heaven, said I
Send the best
That ever took
Lead to its breast.

Upon the word
Upon the right
Rose up a phoenix
Beaming bright.

I raised my gun
I took the sight
My lead unbarred
That breast of white,

Alas for awful
Magic art
The bullet bounced
Into my heart.

The phoenix bled
My heart can not
But heavy sits
Neath leaden shot.

Leave shooting, friend,
Or if you must
Shoot only what
Is mortal dust.

Pray not to Heaven
He stock your bag
Or you may feel
Your vitals sag.

Pray not to Heaven
For heavenly bird
Or Heaven may take you
At your word.

Stevie Smith

In Scotland access has traditionally been easier than in England and Wales though there has never been any absolute *right* of access. Recently however, forestry has made it difficult to gain access to some mountains, while new fencing is spreading rapidly over the hills, some of it electrified deer fencing several feet high. So public access is being reduced.

Antlers and farm shed, Rannoch Moor

Parts of the rich farmland of Grampian Region have been heavily forested with conifers. Near the beautiful beech paths, several hills are covered with funereal forestry.

Farmland near Fettercairn, Angus

For many years Graham Malcolm was an animal-feedstuffs salesman, but became disenchanted because the manufacturers did not have to state what the product contained.

'I don't give my stock anything that I wouldn't eat myself,' says Malcolm who uses semi-organic methods on his 5-acre smallholding, and now has a smokery for bacon and sausages which he sells by mail order. 'I take in bacon and other meats from neighbouring farmers, and since I used to sell feedstuffs to all of them, I know which ones have really good produce.'

In an interview with Derek Cooper on Radio Four's *Food Programme* Malcolm said: 'We have gone back to farming to where it was forty or fifty years ago – it provides a living and a small cash surplus – before it became agribusiness. We don't spurn modern technology where it can help our business – for instance we vacuum pack most of our produce.'

Graham Malcolm's smallholding near Brechin

When the first fish-farms appeared, I thought they were a charming extension to lobster-pots and so on, and a good addition to the difficult economies of remote areas. That was before the big conglomerates moved in: there are now more than 600, more than one in some lochs. Planning authorities have no control as fish-farming is classed as agriculture – it's MAFF again. This colossal expansion has brought pollution problems, and threatens the beauty of the landscape. The salmon are fed a synthetic dye, canthaxanthin, to change their flesh from muddy grey to appetising pink. Anti-biotics and sulphonamides are used, and residues have been found in both salmon and trout. But most damaging of all is Nuvan which is used to eradicate sea-lice, and workers have been rather cavalier with it, ignoring safety precautions; now other means of control are being researched; I even hear that a 'browser' fish which feeds on sea-lice is being investigated. Seals and herons are shot as they eat the fish. Shellfish farmers are resentful as their grounds are encroached on, and sometimes polluted.

It is ironic to hear that as a result of the huge increase of intensive, chemical fish-farming, there is now over-production, and prices are falling, jeopardising jobs; while pollution of the lochs threatens the future of fish-farming itself.

Fish-farming, Loch Ewe, near Gairloch

Gruinard Island seen from the mainland near Gairloch in 1988

In 1942 Gruinard was experimentally infected with anthrax and was out of bounds to the public for nearly fifty years. However, in 1990 the island was officially declared safe by the MoD, although doubts about this 'safety' have been expressed in some quarters.

Fragility of Dusk

The world is stretched so taut and thin
Before the pomps of night begin.
Rain in the air hangs caught like fire,
And every sound a narrow wire
Plucked by fingers out of sight;
And the sky empty, thinned of light;

And night falls crisply flake by flake.
The world is made of stuff so rare,
I think each moment it might break
To dust and vanish in the air
Or, seasoned wood, too dry, might leap
To sudden flame then fall asleep.

E. J. Scovell

Drained forestry land with snow near Lairg, Sutherland

'Why *did* the NCC get its marching orders in Scotland? It was the "Flow Country" which sealed its fate . . . One of the tasks of the new Scottish natural heritage agency will be to investigate all SSSIs and sweep away the dross created by indiscriminate conservation.' (From *Forestry and British Timber*, the magazine for British forestry management.)

Survivors

The last wolf in Scotland
was killed two centuries ago.

I'd like to meet it.

I wouldn't ask
why it opened the throats of deer and
tore mountain hares to pieces.
I wouldn't ask why it howled

in the corries and put one paw
delicately in a mountain torrent.

– It would have nothing to ask me
except, 'Why am I
the last wolf in Scotland?'

I would know what it meant,
for I am the last of my race
as you are, and she, and he.

We would look strangely at each other
before it loped back to its death
and I again put one foot
dangerously into the twentieth century.

Norman MacCaig

New forestry planting near Lairg

'Everything begins in mysticism and ends in
politics.' Charles Péguy

Drains and conifers, near Lairg

Monocultural forestry has resulted in various pests spreading rapidly, especially the pine-beauty moth. Forests are now given an aerial spray annually, mostly at public expense, and possibly hazardous to public health. Our open moorlands have always been a source of delight and inspiration to walkers and artists, and all sorts of people. But now many of the best mountain walks in the highlands have to be approached through the grim ranks of suffocating conifers (see p. 17).

Pine-beauty moth damage, Sutherland

A well-kempt forest begs Our Lady's grace;
Someone is not disgusted, or at least
Is laying bets upon the human race
Retaining enough decency to last;
The trees encountered on a country stroll
Reveal a lot about a country's soul.

A small grove massacred to the last ash,
An oak with heart-rot, give away the show:
This great society is going smash;
They cannot fool us with how fast they go,
How much they cost each other and the gods!
A culture is no better than its woods.

W. H. Auden
from *Bucolics*

Ettrick Valley, Dumfries and Galloway

Outside contractors are often brought in to fell the trees, creating as much havoc and desolation as the forests themselves. In Sweden, clear-cutting is now controlled by county forest boards; they take note of the public's right to enjoy the landscape; paths must not be damaged, and near residential areas extra considerations apply; wildlife must also be taken into account.

Roger Bradley of the Forestry Commission comments: 'The population there is much more adventurous, and they're much more used to using the forests we regard as remote.'

Huge areas of Dumfries and Galloway have been covered in conifers, particularly the Ettrick Valley. Nithsdale, with its ancient Roman fortlet and Roman trackways, has escaped so far.

Smallholding near Lochinver

Clive and Pamela Sheppard run this organic
smallholding on the beautiful Sutherland
coast. Clive Sheppard: 'There is a living to
be made from organic produce, particularly
if you develop a local market for quality
produce.' The rare breeds are fed entirely on
organic produce and are an integral part of
the system.

Rare breeds at Stoer House Nursery, Lochinver

All over the Highlands and Islands there are crofts ruined by the Highland clearances. Now some crofts provide a fragile living, boosted by tourism. However, crofters are again threatened, this time by the poll tax, often as high in remote areas without services and amenities as in cities such as Inverness.

Ruined croft house above Assynt, Sutherland

The ruined path from Lochinver to White Shore Beach

The handsome plaque in the middle of these ruined woods reads: 'This Wood was planted by the Factor of the Duke of Sutherland for the enjoyment of the Community. 1835'

Since 1987, however, the Community cannot enjoy these woods or the popular Ladies' Walk – a mile-long route from Lochinver through the woods to the White Shore Beach.

When the Vestey Estate sold the Culag Hotel on the Pier at Lochinver to the Highland Regional Council so that the busy fishing harbour could expand, timber was harvested and there was subsequent windthrow. The path was obstructed and damaged as well, and at the time of going to press the Council had still not cleared it.

I turn back, and again on nature look
And find clouds, earth, rain, mountains, tree and brook
Different, good in themselves, but not concerned
With our play, no theme's counterpoint, not turned
As cyclorama or revolving stage;
We are their background rather: them no age
Compromises, their hearts can never break
Nor fail at filthy violence; they make
Final truth which no further inference carries;
Glorious like poems, not like commentaries.

Hal Summers
from *At My First Look*

Looking south towards Fisherfield Forest

Some of the most beautiful landscapes in the British Isles are in the Hebrides. But their remoteness poses economic and education problems; there are military pressures such as the much-resisted but now rapidly expanding NATO base at Stornoway; fish-farms are proliferating and though they bring much-needed work, they also bring pollution, threatening traditional fishing grounds which have anyway been over-fished. Over-production causes salmon prices to drop. The future is uncertain, compounded by the poll tax. And stands of deadening forestry plantations are spreading in Harris.

Let's hope the islanders don't have to resort to theme-park tourism, with all-weather pleasure complexes.

Mealista, Lewis

Seilebost, Harris

The Shetland Islands Council was careful to see that environmental damage from North Sea oil was minimised, and Shetland is reasonably unspoiled and relatively prosperous. Access to the hills is free and open, and so far there are no funereal conifer plantations. But the RSPB is puzzling over the decline in bird populations. They are failing to breed, and dying all around Shetland's coasts. The problem seems to be related to food supply, especially sand eels and small fish; the Arctic tern has been the most seriously affected with practically no young during the past six years, and over the last two summers other birds such as puffins and skuas have also failed to breed.

The RSPB says that research is desperately needed. There are unexplained rises of several degrees in coastal water temperatures, possibly due to changing ocean currents. The RSPB is contributing to research, and while more Government funding is needed, the Government has, in fact, scaled down funds for oceanic research.

Drystone walls, Mealista, Lewis

Reflected sun, Grobsness, Shetland

Croft, Mealista, Lewis

There are MoD remains all over the Western Isles, some of the most stunning and unspoilt country we have. 'The buildings were useful when they used them, and they have an absolute obligation to restore the sites when they've finished with them,' says Brian Wilson MP, whose home is in Lewis.

MoD remains

Ex-Ministry of Defence land, Mealista, Lewis

Aird Uig, ex-RAF Camp

'Our main concern when disposing of redundant land is to ensure that it is cleared of explosive materials and other potentially harmful substances. In other respects the property is generally sold in its existing condition, unless it is necessary to remove dangerous buildings or installations. In the specific case to which you refer at Aird Uig, the site was sold as long ago as 1973. It is since it has been in private ownership that it has deteriorated and suffered from the effects of vandalism.' MoD statement

Aird Uig, ex-RAF Camp

learning to love the environment

Apart from going out to the countryside for walks (400 million country walks of more than 2 miles are made each year), growing numbers are drawn to visit stately homes, theme parks, educational farms, and so on. Some of these are beginning to claim a role in educating us about the countryside and our history, with varying degrees of accuracy. Some of the big estates allow school visits, like Beaulieu through its Countryside Education Trust; Chatsworth opens its marvellous parkland, woods and river banks to parties of school-children during the summer months. Theme parks vary from being informative and fun, all the way down to crassly vulgar and a travesty of history.

Many primary schools, like Coombes Infant School near Reading, are doing wonderful environmental work with children, often in difficult inner-city circumstances. As Winchelsea primary school-teacher Cliff Dean said, 'You cannot teach a child to care about the environment until he or she has learned to love it.'

Farm trails are becoming increasingly popular and are one way of diversifying. The city farms give inner-city children a chance to learn about farm animals. The child who has cared for animals on one of these farms will not leave farm gates open in later life – farmers' main complaint against walkers on their land is that they leave gates open, and leave rubbish which may be harmful to farm animals. Many of the London farms are underfunded and under threat as the Inner London Educational Authority grant is withdrawn. Yet they are an excellent use of redundant city space.

Far too little attention is paid to keeping cities attractive: many of our inner-cities, including Camden where I live, are now so filthy and revolting that we have to get out into the country. With inadequate public transport, we clog up the roads in long jams, and contribute to the greenhouse effect. Cities can and should be fine places to be. Our green spaces are always vulnerable to demands for new roads, rail terminals, and even, in the case of Rainham Marshes, on the eastern outskirts of London, for a theme park, even though much of it is an SSSI. The health of the countryside depends on our keeping the cities healthy.

The theme park at Peter de Savary's stately home, Littlecote, specialises in history, with a strong educational bent; on arrival one finds signs stating whether or not it is term time (in which case there will be coach-loads of school-children). There is an 'Elizabethan Tournament of Horses', falconry, and plays; there is a Roman villa and museum, farms and herb gardens, and restaurants where 'waitress service by winsome wenches can be arranged'.

'Superstition abounds at Littlecote and it is advisable not to mock, for the old ways remain in the flowers and the ribbons on the May pole, and in the wild prancing of the Hobby Horse, so beware you visitors from another Time!' (From the Littlecote Souvenir Guide.)

Littlecote

Children's farm, Littlecote

Milton Keynes concrete cow

Dairyland, near Newquay, Cornwall

Dairyland is a working farm where the owners have diversified into tourism. Visitors can visit the rotary milking parlour for the 150 cows, follow a farm trail, visit the country-life museum, farm park, and playground where they can touch and play with the animals. It is attractively designed with a strong educational bias.

Festival of Food and Farming, Hyde Park, 1989

In ASDA's official souvenir programme for the Festival of Food and Farming HRH the Duke of Edinburgh wrote: 'The purpose of the Festival in Hyde Park is to give the inhabitants of the nation's capital a chance to find out where their nourishment comes from and how it reaches their tables.'

In fact, the exhibition fudged all the issues, and dealt in exclusive products such as hand-made cheeses, organically reared animals and lots of whimsy. There was virtually no reference to how current, intensive, chemical farming affects either our food or the countryside. One of the few stalls to reflect the realities of modern farming was the RSPCA's, with heartbreaking film footage about conditions in factory farms and the slaughter of animals. ICI produced a number of sophisticated brochures with PR information about the advantages of chemicals in farming. Otherwise it was, naturally, ice creams all the way.

It was four years before Susan Humphries, Headmistress of Coombes Infant School near Reading, was able to grow anything on the poisoned school grounds after the land had been intensively farmed for years. As she learned to take the town council's leaves in the autumn, to build up fertility in the soil, the children in turn learned about their environment. Fifteen years later flora and fauna flourish: instead of smart approaches to the school, there are 'habitat' patches, and the children's own beans, sunflowers and pumpkins.

Susan Humphries says children's early experiences are extremely powerful, especially up to the age of seven. These children are being given an extraordinary chance to respect and cherish the environment, and the school has recently won many environmental awards.

Habitats at Coombes Infant School, Aborfield, Berkshire

Lunchtime: 'Young children need to be among living things: they will learn respect for life and for the environment,' Susan Humphries, Headmistress

The Kentish Town City Farm is visited by 25–30,000 people each year, including school groups. Many children come each day, and they get invaluable experience in handling the animals, which are often less accessible in the country; there are pony rides, and small organic garden plots. It is also a favourite place for senior citizens watching the children and animals.

The farm was under threat because the abolition of ILEA would cut its funding by 25 per cent; for the time being Camden Education Authority is replacing this grant.

The Kentish Town City Farm

Tablehurst Biodynamic Farm

Tablehurst Biodynamic Farm is part of Emerson College which draws its inspiration from the work of Rudolf Steiner. Students from more than twenty nations attend courses on biodynamic farming, and on rural development programmes for assistance with small-scale growing in depressed areas. The College in their statement about biodynamic farming say: 'A key factor is the adaptation of farming and gardening methods to suit the specific conditions of the natural and social settings. Biodynamics offers a coherent way to achieve soil fertility and increased productivity by the careful use of local resources.' Biodynamics actively seeks to bring in healing measures in the way the soil is fertilized.

In an interview with Derek Cooper on Radio Four's *Food Programme*, Dr Koepf, Director of the Biodynamic School of Agriculture, said that a survey by the Ministry of Agriculture in Stuttgart found that in production levels and also net profit the biodynamics came out well as compared with conventional agribusiness farming. It also benefits the environment and wildlife.

Straw is recycled as a mulch for gooseberries at Tablehurst Biodynamic Farm

The Soil Association is now conducting a ten-year study to compare biodynamic, organic and conventional agribusiness farming.

Although subsidies and high guaranteed prices have encouraged conventional farmers to maximise their yields while polluting the soil and water, there have been no subsidies for organic farmers. MAFF is now paying subsidies to some agribusiness farmers not to use nitrates, but the organic farmers who have never used them get no such subsidies. It takes from two to four years for a farm to gain the Soil Association's approval, and there is no subsidy designed to cover this interim period, when income drops.

In Sweden there is a heavy tax on the use of chemical fertilizers, and this money is used to pay farmers to convert to biodynamic and organic methods. The grants, phased over three years, are given on the basis that the farmer will work biodynamically or organically for at least five years. The scheme is controlled on behalf of the Government by the two existing biodynamic and organic agencies.

Derek Cooper said: 'Both biodynamic and organic farming are based on the principle that the land should be treated with respect. Chemical farming puts the crop first and the long-term health of the soil very far behind. Until we as consumers express some interest in how our fruit and vegetables are grown, then the environmentally conscious kind of farming will remain a fringe activity,' (see p. 15).

inner-city space

Camley Street is a magical place. Reclaimed from an abandoned coal-yard and rubbish dumps in 1983 by the London Wildlife Trust, it is probably the most visited nature reserve in Britain, and wildlife thrives in this tiny park, overshadowed by King's Cross and the gasworks. It is booked up for school visits, two each day, for months ahead, and at the weekends, local Londoners, adults and children, go to get a breath of air and observe the wildlife, and perhaps do a bit of pond-dipping. Its value cannot be measured in money.

Camley Street has been under threat ever since the new King's Cross Terminal was first mooted. Even though the Channel Tunnel routes are being reconsidered, British Rail is determined to construct a cut-and-cover tunnel through Camley Street. There are other ways of doing this, but they are more expensive. After the cut-and-cover, British Rail proposes to let the LWT have the park back, but the question is when? What's more, there would only be about 3 feet of soil over the tunnel, so it would be impossible to plant trees, which flourish there now.

The LWT writes: 'If this children's nature reserve is destroyed for the sake of minor engineering convenience or an extra percentage profit, it will not only be a tragedy for Britain's capital, but an indication that the ''greening'' of politics has not yet reached the boardrooms of BR and our leading development companies.'

Camley Street Natural Park

Kirkstall Nature Reserve in Leeds was the only reserve in Britain to receive a European Year of the Environment Award from Prince Charles in 1988. At the same time Leeds City Development Corporation, encouraged by Nicholas Ridley, together with Mountleigh Northern Developments, had outline planning permission to turn the whole of the Kirkstall Valley into a business park, and were offering to include a dinosaur theme park. There were furious objections and the dinosaurs were extinguished.

Since then there have been fourteen other proposals; the plans have been in limbo as the developers could not agree, due to problems with costs. An entirely separate plan, the Kirkstall Valley Campaign, was from a community-development organisation and would cost very little to implement. This would retain the existing playing-fields, fish-ponds, nature reserves and the allotments on grade one agricultural land. There would be a recycling centre for Leeds which would yield horticultural compost and methane gas to be used for a combined heat and power scheme. There would also be plenty of scope for office, retail and light industrial development, as well as space for 'commercial' leisure, restaurants and hotels. While there are serious financial questions hanging over the commercial developers' proposals, 'the community plan could be done tomorrow and has been welcomed by a variety of national and local environmental organisations,' says Dr John Illingworth of the Department of Bio-chemistry at Leeds University, who is also a Leeds City Councillor.

This story of developers whose plans would deprive the local community of their green and thriving Kirkstall Valley, in inner-city Leeds, turning it into a business park with 5,000 parking spaces, reminds me of nineteenth-century enclosures, and of a passage I read in *The Bleak Age* by J. I. and Barbara Hammond: the subject of playgrounds was brought before Parliament in 1833 by a select committee to consider the 'deficiency of public walks and Places of Exercise'. The facts were presented: 'As respects those employed in the three great Manufactures of the Kingdom, Cotton, Woollen, and Hardware, creating annually an immense Property, no provision has been made to afford them the means of healthy exercise or cheerful amusement with their families on their Holidays or days of rest.'

Things haven't changed much. It is crucial that provision is made for recreation within the cities – it could reduce the miserable exodus of people trying to find the countryside on congested roads at the weekends. It has always been, and still is, the urban green areas which are most vulnerable to loss by development.

Kirkstall Nature Reserve, in inner-city Leeds

Salts Mill in Saltaire now houses a Hockney Museum

One problem with our countryside is that many of our cities have been allowed to crumble into squalor, while developers are always after the next 'greenfield' site, often offering a 'planning gain' – a bribe – of some kind in return for permission. In West Germany some cities, like Cologne, have been made so delightful that people pour *in*, not out, at weekends.

One man who has shown how city dereliction can be reversed is Ernest Hall. When the huge Crossley Carpet mills closed down in 1982, it looked like disaster for Halifax. But Ernest Hall, who is a professional musician as well as having been a property developer, bought the mills and now Dean Clough is a thriving and most attractive industrial park, together with artists' studios, art galleries, art collections and wine bars.

Dean Clough's success has revitalised Halifax so that unemployment has been enormously reduced, business confidence restored, and cultural life revitalised, while property values have gone up too.

Dean Clough Industrial Park, Halifax

Badbury Rings, National Trust, Dorset

Erosion repair with duckboards, Pennine Way

Badbury Rings in Dorset is free of charge to the public. When the National Trust acquired the rings from the Bankes Estate in 1982 there were serious erosion problems. The upkeep for sites like Badbury Rings comes from endowment funds, general funds, and Countryside Commission grants.

Alan Mattingly, Director of the Ramblers' Association, writes: 'The impact of ramblers' boots has been identified as only a minor cause of moorland erosion and vegetation loss in peat-covered upland areas. Overgrazing by sheep and air pollution are the main culprits. But along some stretches of *very* heavily used paths, such as the Pennine Way and Lyke Wake Walk, erosion by trampling is a serious and growing problem. Unfortunately, the cure that is attempted sometimes looks worse than the problem itself.'

Alan Mattingly:

'The use of market forces to solve environmental problems has been widely canvassed since the publication of the Pearce report, *Blueprint for a Green Economy*. This theme is found, for example, in arguments that walkers should be charged for access to eroded upland footpaths. This, the argument has it, would both curb demand and thus reduce impact, and would generate money for path repair. This is a specious and dangerous line of reasoning.

'In the first place it would simply not be practical to charge people for entry to the hills, except in very limited circumstances. The cost of establishing toll booths, paying staff to collect the charges, and paying "path policemen" to ensure that walkers do not creep on to the path from other points of access, would generally be prohibitive.

'Second, most popular upland paths are highways in law. People are already paying for their upkeep through rates and taxes.

'Third, public expenditure in recreation is rightly regarded as a good investment in the health and well-being of the nation's population. Given that walking is one of the most popular and beneficial forms of outdoor recreation, public expenditure on providing and maintaining the facilities which our recreation needs (particularly properly cared-for footpaths) is well worthwhile.

'Indeed, it is plain that country walking is a grossly under-funded recreation. Despite being highly cost-effective (the net cost to the public purse of someone taking a long walk in the country is 3½ pence; that for a visit to an indoor sports facility is 60p), expenditure on rights of way in England and Wales is, at £14 million per year, minuscule compared to total local authority spending on tourism, leisure and recreation (£1 billion).

'But the most important argument against charging is an ethical one. It is one thing for a landowner to charge a fee for a particular facility, such as a car park, which he has incurred expenditure in providing. It is quite another proposition for an owner to attempt to extract money from people who simply set foot on his land, without intruding on his privacy, or doing any damage to crops or livestock.

'Over most of the highlands of Scotland and in some parts of the uplands of England and Wales, there has been a long tradition of freedom of access to uncultivated land. It is essential that this is not undermined by any precedent which charging for access to upland footpaths would create.

'So what should be done?

'For reasons spelt out earlier, far more public resources should be allocated for the work of restoring upland paths and of maintaining them in a stable and walkable condition. More research is needed into effective and environmentally acceptable methods of restoring eroded paths in the diverse soil and vegetation conditions found in the British uplands. Some of the huge amounts of public money which have been poured into supporting intensive agriculture in recent years should be redirected so that farmers are rewarded for protecting the environment instead of destroying it, and for looking after footpaths instead of obstructing them. In the uplands this should mean financial incentives for, among other things, agreements and contracts to help look after upland footpaths. Provided that an adequate standard of work was maintained, farmers could act as agents of highway authorities in carrying out the latters' duty to maintain rights of way.

'Pressure can also be reduced by methods other than charging. For example, it may be appropriate to restrict the amount of car-parking space close to the start of some heavily used paths. It may also be wise, especially on peak tourist days in summer, to close certain roads to motor traffic, except that requiring access to local houses and farms. Others seeking access to the area concerned would be obliged to undertake the "long walk in".

'Pressure can be reduced by offering people alternatives. Many may go for a day walk on the Pennine Way, for example, simply because they know it is there and because they are unaware of any equally attractive and accessible alternatives. Local authorities, national park authorities and tourist boards could do much to make such alternatives more widely known.

'Publishers of guide-books to popular mountain areas should be careful not to publicise over-used footpaths. Restraint should also be exercised by organisers of large-scale sponsored walks. They should avoid the use of eroded paths and plan routes on tracks which can withstand the impact of large numbers of people.

'Whatever measures are adopted to deal with path erosion, it is essential that such measures are based firmly on the policy that public access on foot to wild areas is desirable, should be allowed, and should only be restricted where there are sound, demonstrable reasons for so doing.

'And the problem of path erosion must be kept in its proper context. For in the uplands of Britain there are threats to the environment which are far more damaging than anything which walkers' boots alone may cause. Conifer afforestation, mineral extraction, tourism complexes, urban and industrial development, intensive agriculture and the neglect of ancient woodland have damaged, and continue to damage, upland landscapes and wildlife habitats to a degree which makes footpath erosion almost pale into insignificance.'

Erosion repair with man-made materials, Pennine Way

'Free the Stones', Stonehenge, solstice 1988

Nightguard, Stonehenge

The Mother

Slowly, slowly, she turns over through the night,
Turns her lovely face towards the morning light,
Always turning, turning, turning,
On her long and endless journey through the sky.

Slowly, slowly, she turns over through the day,
Flowers bloom and seed and die and fade away,
Seasons turning, turning, turning,
Till tomorrow's just a memory of today.

Virgin water tumbling, tumbling down the hill,
First the storm and then the time when all is still.
All will follow, follow, follow,
All in balance when the earth does as she will.

Who invades the sky to bring the goddess down?
Who's laid poison in her body, in her bones?
The earth is trembling, trembling, trembling –
Is she waiting for the deadly, final wound?

Wanton child, beware the power of tide,
Learn to answer to the mother's warning cry!
Learn to follow, follow, follow,
Live with all that live on earth – or all will die.

Peggy Seeger

The Stone Circle at Avebury is owned by the National Trust (though the stones themselves are in the care of English Heritage). It has, so far, escaped the fate suffered by Stonehenge, though there are problems with wear. Although until recently it has occasionally been possible to enjoy its tranquillity and harmony in relative solitude, during the last couple of years serious threats have emerged. A property developer has opened an Elizabethan theme park in the

Avebury

Manor House, and huge numbers of people come in fleets of coaches to watch the jousts, Victorian steam engine rallies and so on. They then take a stroll around the stones. Avebury is thus in danger of becoming a theme park with semi-detached stone circle. Many of these visitors would never have dreamt of coming to Avebury, and because of these new throngs of people, attracted by the flotsam of history, Avebury may eventually have to be fenced off for its own protection. But this will be difficult and even uglier than Stonehenge since there is a village in the middle of the circle, which is also crossed by a trunk road. Thus the true value of the Avebury Stone Circle may soon be lost as at Stonehenge. Once again 'marketing' will be the damaging force, albeit marketing of the theme park in the case of Avebury.

Glastonbury Tor

the dance moves in us
we turn to the measure of stars
      of the hidden waters
we follow the bird's flight
     and the song
          always beyond us
the shifting of leaves is our music
our pattern the shadow of cloud
we dance to the sun
on the white hill we dance
we dance to the stillness
      at the heart of the dance

Frances Horovitz

Glastonbury has survived the trampling of
many feet, and many festivals.

Glastonbury Tor, owned by the National Trust

South-west from Dunkery Beacon on the National Trust's Exmoor land

Farewell, you Northern hills,
You mountains all, goodbye!
Moorland and stony ridges,
Crags and peaks, goodbye!
Glyder Fach, farewell,
Cul Beig, Scafell,
Cloud-bearing Suilven.
Sun-warmed rock and the cold
Of Bleaklow's frozen sea,
The snow and the wind and the rain
Of hills and mountains.
Days in the sun and the tempered wind,
And the air like wine,
And you drink and you drink till you're drunk
On the joy of living.

          . . . . . .

Take me to some high place
Of heather, rock and ling;
Scatter my dust and ashes,
Feed me to the wind.
So that I will be
Part of all you see,
The air you are breathing.
I'll be part of the curlew's cry
And the soaring hawk,
The blue milkwort
And the sundew hung with diamonds.
I'll be riding the gentle wind
That blows through your hair;
Reminding you how we shared
In the joy of living.

Ewan MacColl
from *The Joy of Living*

LIST OF PHOTOGRAPHS

Whereas most of the pictures in this book were taken specifically for it, those on the following pages are from earlier books:
pp. 37, 47 (from *The Secret Forest of Dean*);
pp. 34, 49, 106 (from *The Saxon Shore Way*);
p. 61 (from *Romney Marsh*); pp. 178, 187, 188 (from *The National Trust Book of Wessex*).

FURTHER ACKNOWLEDGMENTS
AND FURTHER READING

further acknowledgments

The author and publishers are grateful to the following for permission to reproduce the poems quoted in the text: Bloodaxe Books in association with Enitharmon Press, 'Winter Woods' and 'Glastonbury Tor' from *Collected Poems* by Frances Horovitz (edited by Roger Garfitt); Macmillan Publishers Ltd, 'At Day-close in November' by Thomas Hardy; Hal Summers for his poem 'The Yorkshire Moors'; Peggy Seeger and Felix de Wolfe for 'The Vandals', two verses from 'The Joy of Living' (a valedictory message) by Ewan MacColl and 'The Mother' by Peggy Seeger, all © Ewan MacColl Ltd; Phil Vallack for his poem 'Refuse Cruise'; Methuen London, 'The God of War' from *Poems 1913–1956* by Bertolt Brecht (translated by Michael Hamburger); Peters Fraser & Dunlop Group Ltd, 'A German Requiem' by James Fenton; Faber and Faber Ltd, 'Augury' from *Wintering Out* by Seamus Heaney, and two verses from 'Bucolics' from *Collected Poems* by W. H. Auden; Ted Hughes for his poem 'What the Serpent Said to Adam'; Allison & Busby, 'All The World's Beauty' from *For Beauty Douglas: Collected Poems* by Adrian Mitchell; Chatto & Windus Ltd, 'Landscape and I' and 'Survivors' from *Collected Poems* by Norman MacCaig; James MacGibbon (literary executor), 'Es War Einmal' from *The Collected Poems of Stevie Smith* (Penguin Twentieth Century Classics); Carcanet Press Ltd, 'Fragility of Dusk' from *Collected Poems* by E. J. Scovell; J. M. Dent & Sons Ltd, one verse from 'At My First Look' from *Hinterland* by Hal Summers.

further reading

John Blunden and Nigel Curry (editors), *A People's Charter?*, Countryside Commission and HMSO, 1989.

Geoffrey Cannon, *The Politics of Food*, Century, 1987.

David Crouch and Colin Ward, *The Allotment: Landscape and Culture*, Faber & Faber, 1988.

Nicholas Humphrey, *Four Minutes to Midnight* (the Bronowski Memorial Lecture), Menard Press, 1981.

Richard Jefferies, *The Pageant of Summer*, Quartet Books, 1979.

Penelope Lively, *The Presence of the Past: An Introduction to Landscape History*, Collins, 1975.

Richard Mabey, *In a Green Shade: Essays on Landscape*, Century Hutchinson, 1983.

Geoffrey Moorhouse, *The Other England*, Penguin Books, 1964.

North Sea Action Group, *A Case for Treatment for those in Peril by the Sea*, Norfolk Friends of the Earth, 1989.

Ann Holt (editor), *Making Tracks: A Celebration of 50 Years of the Ramblers' Association*, Ramblers' Association, 1985.

Ruth Rendell and Colin Ward, *Undermining the Central Line: Giving Government Back to the People*, Chatto & Windus, 1989.

E. F. Schumacher, *Small is Beautiful*, Blond & Briggs, 1973.

Marion Shoard, *The Theft of the Countryside*, Temple Smith, 1980.

Marion Shoard, *This Land is our Land*, Paladin Books, 1987.

Tom Stephenson, *Forbidden Land*, Manchester University Press, 1989.

Steve Tompkins, *The Theft of the Hills*, Ramblers' Association, 1986.

Caroline Walker and Geoffrey Cannon, *The Food Scandal*, Century, 1984.